JD'S

Inspirational MOMENTS

JANINE DAVIS

Book Cover Design by Nimra Bukhari

1 edition 2023

DISCLAIMER

The information provided within this book is for general informational purposes only. While we try to keep the information up-to-date and correct, there are no representations or warranties, express or implied, about the completeness, accuracy, reliability, suitability or availability with respect to the information, products, services, or related graphics contained in this book for any purpose. Any use of the methods described within this book are the author's personal thoughts. They are not intended to be a definitive set of instructions for this project. You may discover there are other methods and materials to accomplish the same end result.

CONTENTS

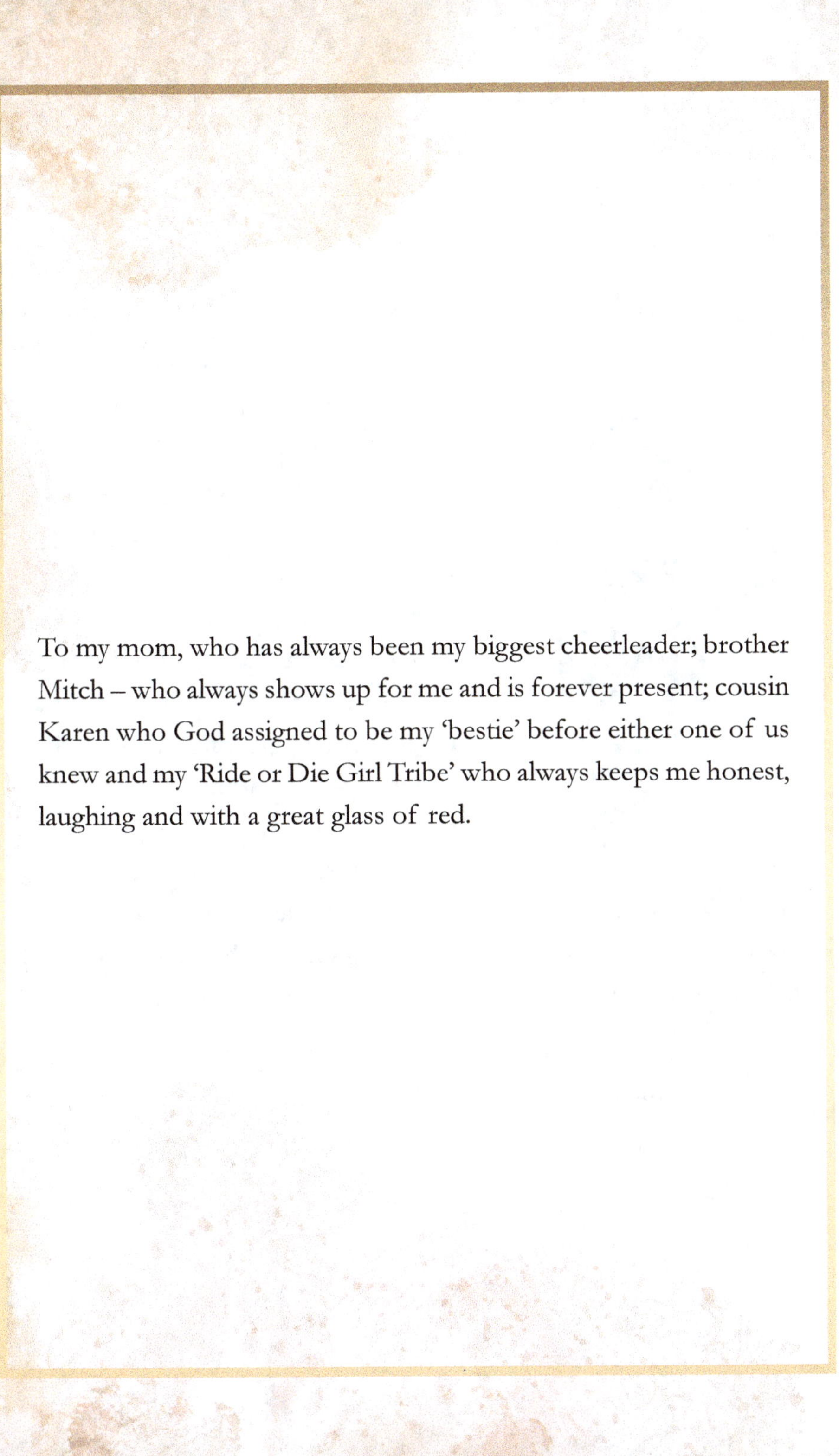

To my mom, who has always been my biggest cheerleader; brother Mitch – who always shows up for me and is forever present; cousin Karen who God assigned to be my 'bestie' before either one of us knew and my 'Ride or Die Girl Tribe' who always keeps me honest, laughing and with a great glass of red.

MY WHY

I'm a southern girl from Greensboro, NC who started life timid and shy. I actually 'dropped out' of kindergarten. I've learned that was only the beginning of my 'living' my testimony. Alot has happened since then. In college is where I gained self-confidence. Today, that has led me to my own radio show in one of the fastest-growing cities in the country — Charlotte. I've made this my home and while here I have grown intellectually, emotionally and spiritually. I've tapped into the importance of purpose. Which brings me to this book. My hope is it gives you the inspiration and clarity it has given me. And that it will help you land in the place where you will flourish in purpose.

Keep thriving!

CHAPTER ONE

Where Is My Subscription?

Over the holiday, my family and I watched a ton of movies. My cousin was especially excited because with her smart TV, she could see the apps for several premiums channels - HBO, Showtime, Starz. Our plan was to watch "Power" on Starz.

So when my cousin opened the app, it asked for her login information – which she didn't have. I explained, "You only have the app, you will not have the service unless you subscribe to it!" Instantly, the light bulb went off.

And for me too, when I had my devotion today I read John 15:5 – when Jesus says

"I am the vine, you are the branches. When we're joined, the relation is intimate; harvest is abundant. Separated, you CAN'T produce a thing."

Sometimes in life we can think we have it all together; got it all like my cousin and her premium channels. Having the apps, were not enough because she didn't have the service. I'm reminded, to get God's goodness, I have to subscribe to Him and be connected.

Now, go be Great!

Case Of A Bad Driver

I was in a grocery store parking lot yesterday finishing up a call. I had backed into the parking space. While on the phone, I noticed a few cars parked directly across from me. The driver seemed to back out so slowly. It was an elderly lady with a Prius who took forever to back out.

Then a similar incident occurred with another woman in a jeep. She almost hit me while trying to back out!

And then another driver did the same thing!

I'm thinking, "Why can't people drive?!!" I got off the phone, and out of my car and noticed — I wasn't completely backed in the parking space.

My front end was sticking out and THAT'S why people had creeped around ME! Trying NOT to hit ME! My devotion today hit home.

Matthew 7:5 says "First remove the plank from your own eye, then you can see clearly to remove the speck from you brother's eye."

God simply reminded me – check yourself first, Janine before getting an attitude. It might just be YOU who is in the wrong.

Now, go be Great!

Do Different

I called a girlfriend just to check in to see if she'd gotten in her exercise. We're both on a journey to get and stay healthy. I suspected she had NOT gotten in her walk. I was right. She said, "Girl, I've got to get this weight off!!"

Then I said to her, THEN DO IT. Put on our workout gear leave the house and WALK!"

I thought about what I said to her and said to myself – which is 'I want 2021 to be different. " But, it can only be different, if I DO DIFFERENT. Like with my girlfriend, our weight is NOT going to magically 'go away.' We have to DO DIFFERENT.

My devotion today reminded me that God wants me to DO DIFFERENT, too.

Ephesians 4:22 says 'throw off your old sinful nature and your former way of life…"

I'm reminded I CAN DO DIFFERENT. Let go of the old Janine, and trust God to help me be the NEW.

Now, go be Great!

It's Dark In Here

When I went into my bathroom this morning, I flicked on the light switch and one of my lights went out. I didn't have an extra one, so I was forced to operate in a dimly lit bathroom. Have you ever tried to get ready or put on make up in a dimly lit bathroom? Not the best.

When I had my devotion today, I thought about operating in a dimly lit space – like the dark time our country is in right now. And how hard it was. In my bathroom, I'm thinking, 'all I need is the ONE light bulb to make the difference.' In life, I think about God. And how HE alone makes the difference.

John 12:35 & 36 says "…the light is among you. If you walk in darkness, you don't know where you're going. But you have the light. Believe in it."

I'm reminded in these dark times, just like in my dimly lit bathroom, God IS STILL THE LIGHT. And with Him, I don't have to operate in darkness.

Now, go be Great!

I've Got Mail!

Over the holiday, I was determined to clean out some of my emails. There were 5,000! Janine come on! Anyway, I told myself I just need to stay focused and DO IT. Well, I did it. I trimmed them down to 34 emails.

And boy, did I feel so much better. I actually felt lighter to have cleared out all the junk. But, cleaning out my email felt a lot like fighting against negative forces. Just the mere act of having to take time to clear out email then on top of that deciding "Do I keep this?" "Will I need this later?" "Is this really junk?"

During my devotion, I thought about finally clearing out my emails. And how good it felt to get rid of the junk to reveal what was really important. I thought just like in life. At times I have to 'go through' to get to the blessings of God. So, I'm reminded - the beauty of 'going through' (even with my emails) is the satisfaction of knowing God is there to SEE ME through.

Now, go be Great!

Where's The Money?

I got an alert on my phone this morning saying this billionaire who ran a casino in Las Vegas had passed away. I'd never heard of him, but apparently he'd helped change the landscape in Vegas and gave millions to Republicans. Dead at 87.

I thought about that man's death during my devotion today —

Proverbs 11:4 "Your riches won't help you on Judgment Day, only righteous counts then."

I thought he was a BILLIONAIRE. He had financial security and just like that GONE. I thought all the 'security' in the world doesn't matter if I don't have a relationship with God.

That's a security that outlasts ANY AND EVERYTHING. I'll admit — I DO have my moments when I'm thinking 'God, I don't have enough — or I need more this or that.' I get focused on the material things. But, God reminded me the same attention I pay to 'wanting and accumulating those things', I need to place my TRUST in Him. No need to worry about financial security, Janine. Stay God-centered.

Now, go be Great!

When There's Too Much Noise

I woke up this morning to the sounds of a steady thump. It was my neighbor above me – working out. Apparently jumping rope. Ugh! Then soon after that I hear galloping down the hallway and the shouts of "Stop! Come here! Good boy!" My neighbor and her dog.

I'm thinking – Ugh! They get on my nerves! I just wanna be in my quiet. In my quiet, my devotion and God was speaking to me. Janine - instead of criticizing and condemning, you should show mercy. It's in the bible –

Luke 11:4 "Forgive our sins as we forgive those who sin against us."
Or Ephesians 4:2 "Be patient with each other."

People have quirks. People can irritate you with their habits. But God says I'm supposed to show mercy to my enemies, people I don't agree with or like. I'm reminded, show mercy Janine. Like God shows me. And forgive people even those who irritate me like my NOISEY neighbors.

Now, go be Great!

What Am I Looking For?

Have you ever lost a favorite thing? And you go crazy trying to find it? Like I lost one of my favorite pairs of earrings – they are shoulder dusters. I got them from The Limited years ago and they're still poppin!

Except, I lost one getting in my car the other day. I looked everywhere in my car – the seats, the door side pockets. I looked in the parking garage, followed my steps back to my unit. I looked in my closet. I was determined to find my earring. I finally found it! It got stuck on my sweater underneath my coat!

When I had my devotion today, I was thinking about the vim and vigor I had looking for my earring. And I thought – that's the same way God wants me to seek Him. In fact, He says in

Jeremiah 29:13, "When you come looking for me, you'll find me. When you get serious about finding me & want it more than anything else… I'll turn things around for you."

I'm reminded, just like looking for my earring, I need to SEEK GOD with all I've got. The return will be worth it.

Now, go be Great!

Am I Settling?

I may have mentioned my bathroom light going out not too log ago and how I had to manage in very dim light. Well, thankfully I have a new bulb. My electrician friend had to change out the entire light fixture and suggested I get an LED light bulb! And boy is it bright!! I thought I was seeing before but NOW—I CAN SEE EVERYTHING, EXTRA CLEAR.

I thought how did I ever see before? Apparently, I was just getting by. Kind of like I do sometimes BEFORE turning it over to God. I think I'm doing okay. I'm muddling through. But then I think – why muddle through, Janine when God can cause a breakthrough?

My devotion this morning talked about that very thing. How God still hears me when I have faith in Him.

Matthew 21:22 says , "If you believe, you will receive whatever you ask for in prayer."

I'm reminded, don't settle for dim light when God has a LED light for you. Just believe. God's got it!

Now, go be Great!

What Am I Rushing For?

I've been mapping out my goals for the next three months and even thinking about goals for the year. And when I went to review them the other day, I realized I'm off my schedule. A few things I'm supposed to make happen, I haven't yet.

I'm thinking to myself 'I got deadlines! I gotta get it poppin', JD!!' When I got up this morning for my quiet time, I thought "No, I don't have to get it poppin'– not right now." And my devotion helped confirm that.

Proverbs 2:6 says "For the Lord gives skillful and godly wisdom."

It's the wisdom that hit home for me. I realized God wants me to use wisdom and not operate on emotions. When I have wisdom, then comes patience. I'm hearing God say "Calm down. Stop rushing. Don't act in haste." I'm reminded to sit back for a minute and WAIT to see where God moves me next.

Now, go be Great!

Posting The Perfect Picture

I was scrolling through my socials the other night. You know you wanna see how many likes, follows and new comments you have. We all do it. And if we are really being honest, we are all narcissistic in some way.

I have one friend who will take a picture and then spend another 10 minutes filtering, editing, highlighting to post the perfect picture. When I think about it, it's a crazy obsession. Like everybody wants to be LIKED, get approval. But, when I read my devotion today, I realized I don't need to get approval on instagram or Facebook.

Psalm 37:5 & 6 says , "When I open up before God, keep nothing back. God validates my life and HE gives me a stamp of approval."

I'm reminded, having likes or follows on my socials is nice, but having God's approval is all I really need.

Now, go be Great!

Am I Doing Enough Good?

I saw a post on Girl Talk's instagram the other day. I started Girl Talk almost 20 years ago and even though I stepped down as Executive Director last year, the post I saw made me smile. It was of some of the girls reciting the Girl Talk pledge.

I was so proud and happy to see my vision become a reality – seeing girls empowered. I thought – and I'm not being braggadocios — that's a good deed and God can say well done, Janine.

In my mind, I'm thinking "on to the next good deed." But after reading my devotion, I realized I had it all wrong.

Romans 10:13 says "Everyone who calls on the Lords name will be saved."

Not only people doing good deeds get saved. In other words, doing good isn't good enough when it comes to God. I don't have to work my way into heaven. God has already given me the gift of grace. I'm reminded, to get to heaven all I need to do is BELIEVE IN HIM!

Now, go be Great!

My Garage Door Is Open

I was coming home and about to enter the parking garage. I like to push the button on the garage door opener a little early so once I get to the garage door entrance, I won't have to stop. I can just roll right in. And I did.

And I thought about me just rolling in through the garage door – I thought I was just as confident that door was going to open I didn't stop. I didn't stop because I had clicked the button on the garage door opener. I did all of that without hesitation, so sure it would open up. And it did.

But my devotion today reminded me I need to be that self-assured, that confident, that full of belief when it comes to God.

James 1:5 says ask BOLDLY, BELIEVINGLY, WITHOUT A SECOND THOUGHT.

It says you can't worry through your prayers. I'm reminded, make the ask to God and keep rolling – God is ready and waiting to open the door.

Now, go be Great!

Why Am I Up?

I woke up fully alert around 5:30 this morning, I don't know why, but the last time that happened I think God was trying to tell me something.

Anyway, I immediately started reading my devotion. I received my devotion in three places. 1 – my inbox where Dianna Hobbs who talked about a need or desire that hasn't happened yet. 2 – instagram where influencer Tabitha Brown talked about it taking 42 years for her dream to become a reality and 3 – another inbox message – this one from Pastor Rick Warren who said let God's word comfort and energize you to keep going.

And when I thought about it – all 3 places had a message. Don't give up. Don't stop believing. Don't stop having faith.

James 4:6 essentially says 'Don't be proud. Humble yourself. Give yourself completely to God.'

I thought – ok God I get the message.

Now, go be Great!

What's The Forecast?

I was so looking forward to it being sunny and 70 the other day, because the weather forecasters said so. But, we didn't get sunshine. Instead, it was gray, gloomy and wet – all day.

Then forecasters called for more rain and even some snow in the mountains. When I woke up this morning – JUST THE OPPOSITE. Crystal clear skies, I thought…the forecasters got it wrong again. For the past few days, I'd planned my day around them – get work done on my car, go for a run.

When I had my devotion, I thought I do that , too. I try to forecast what is going to happen in my life. Like weather forecasters I'm SO SURE it'll be a certain way. But,

Proverbs 3 says 'Trust God from the bottom on your heart & don't try to figure out everything on your own. God keeps you on track."

I'm reminded, to trust GOD He's the ONLY forecaster in my life.

Now, go be Great!

When I Have To Force Quit

I opened my laptop this morning and noticed it was running a bit slower than usual. Then I realized I had several programs still open, so I closed them. On the Mac, to close programs you have to do what's called a "force quit."

I had several "force quits" I had to activate. While doing that, I thought about how I sometimes apply "force quits" in my life. Like when buying my place uptown. I didn't wait on God. I did a "force quit", took matters into my own hands & thought I found the spot. Later learned the builder had a ton of lawsuits pending because of construction issues. That wasn't God's plan. His plan – a brand new construction for me that would eventually almost double in value.

My devotion today –

Isaiah 55:18 says "My thoughts are nothing like your thoughts. My ways are far beyond anything you could imagine."

I'm reminded…my way will always be inferior to God's plan. So, I'll wait & go with God.

Now, go be Great!

There's No Permanent Damage

I was on my bed the other day eating some cherries – oooh they were good. Anyway, I had them on a paper towel, but left them there to get up and go in another room. I came back and some of the juice from the cherries had gotten on my blanket. Ugh!

Anyway, I got some cleanser and cold water to get out the stain and kept my fingers crossed that my blanket wouldn't be permanently damaged. Thankfully, it wasn't. The stain was gone.

I thought about that "stain" & damaging my blanket when I read my devotion today. Sometimes I think when I sin, I damage or stain my relationship with God. But, in

Isaiah 1:18 God says "No matter how deep the stain of your sins, I can take it out & make you as clean as snow."

I'm reminded, when I sin there's no permanent damage with God – He says just come back to Him. He can restore me.

Now, go be Great!

When I Can't

I got an email this morning requesting some edits to a project I had done. In fact, I was up late working on this project to make sure it was perfect!! It was, according to the client, EXCEPT…

I was on the verge of complaining…out loud. But in my head, I was screaming. So I decided to just stop and breathe for a minute and think. I thought "is it really that big of a deal, Janine? You can make the change in 10 minutes."

In my devotion (that I so needed) – this verse spoke directly to me.

Philippians 2:14-15 says "Do everything without complaining or arguing so that no one can criticize you."

And then I followed up with

1st Thessalonians 5 "Give thanks in all circumstances…it's God's will for you."

I am reminded very simply: Be grateful. Don't complain.

Now, go be Great!

To Go Or Wait

I was at an intersection earlier this week where there was construction. I was waiting to get a signal from the construction worker on whether to go or not. But, he wasn't the best at hand signals. I didn't know whether to go or wait. It was confusing.

All I needed was a clear signal and fast. Kind of like I am when I need guidance from God. And He doesn't seem to answer me quickly enough. But my devotion today asked the real question. What do I need to hear God's voice?

Evangelist joyce Meyer says a couple of things could be blocking me from hearing God, 1) a clear pathway — do I have sin in my life? 2) My own desires are superseding God's will for me.

I 'm reminded, to hear from God, I need to be persistent in prayer. And I need to be patient & not rush ahead of Him. His signals are clear.

Now, go be Great!

I Am Weak

I had a massage recently that was amazing. Shout out to massage therapist Monica! Anyway, while I was on the table waiting for her to return to the room, I could feel my muscles tense from the weeks and months of life. I had time to focus on – just relaxing.

And I did just that. Eighty minutes later, I felt like a noodle. I was soooo relaxed, muscles not tense. I wasn't sure I could drive home. I'm thinking – Ahhh, just what I needed.

I didn't have a care in the world – after a massage. But, during my devotion today I thought Jesus can have the same impact on you, Janine. You can feel free, no tension. 2nd Corinthians 12 talks about taking your limitations like (stress, abuse, accidents) in stride and letting Jesus take over. It says

"His grace is enough. It's all I need…the weaker I get, the stronger I become."

I'm reminded…God can be my massage therapist 24/7. I just need to let Him.

Now, go be Great!

I Was Stuck On A Single Lane Road

I was out early this morning and on my way back home, I took a side street – with just the single lane. After I saw the construction truck in front of me, I sighed and thought "This is gonna be a long one."

It was a dump truck with a flat bed. One construction worker was on the bed of the truck scooping out mulch to another construction worker who was putting it around the trees. I'm thinking, 'I'm stuck. I'm on a single lane road, I can't back up, can't divert and take another road. All I can do is wait."

So I did. I waited. I breathed and I was quiet. I realized in that moment – God was teaching me something. Here I was once again, in a hurry to get home. But God said, wait, slow down, relax. I'm guiding the ship. I'm reminded, stop looking for shortcuts. Stop fighting the wait. Just wait on God.

Now, go be Great!

When It's Just Okay

Yesterday ended up being kind of a laid back day for me. Of course, I did my radio show from my crib, but afterwards there were no Zoom calls, no conference calls, no production. I handled my emails, but I settled in – just being with me.

And I was clean-faced. No make up, no lashes, just some lip balm, sweats and a tee. And I was okay. I read my devotion and

1st Peter 5:6 and 7 says it's okay to be okay, too. "

So be content with who you are, and don't put on airs. God's hand is on you…"

After reading it, I felt a surge of relief. I thought – it's okay NOT to be EXTRA. God's not into all of that.

First Peter 5 says it – "He takes delight in just plain people."

I thought I'm as plain as it gets today. And I was reminded, and that's okay with God. He's still got me.

Now, go be Great!

When The Vacation Ends...

You know one of the things I loved most about my recent vacation? The FREEDOM of NOT 'managing' anything. No thought-provoking decision. Just BEING. It was GREAT! But what did I do when I returned? Thinking about life; strategizing.

Then I thought Janine, here you go again. Trying to act like God, trying to control circumstances, my future, etc. My devotion today helped me get back on track.

Ephesians 4:22-24 says I'm meant to "take on an entirely new way of life – a God fashioned-life…a renewed life from the inside…where God reproduces His character in you."

God doesn't want me to become a god. He wants me to become GODLY. He wants me to develop his values and his character.

I'm reminded the freedom I felt on vacation – just BEING is a character trait God wants me to develop. That means trusting, obeying & feeling FREE to allow God to lead.

Now, go be Great!

I'm Changing

I had to pull a long day yesterday. In fact, my workday went into the night -- not getting home until around 10pm. And at one point, I was home long enough to eat. Then went right back out to finish my work. I was determined to get it all done – and get it done right!

But, you know what I noticed after I finished? I've changed. Not that I'm tooting my own horn, but I could remember a time not long ago when there was NO WAY I would have gotten home, THEN LEFT BACK OUT after 7pm to GO BACK TO WORK! Who does that?

Apparently I do and with God's help. In my devotion today –

Philippians 2:13 says "God is working in you, giving you the desire and power to do what pleases him."

I realize the behavior I could never imagine myself exhibiting, was GOD. And it was subtle. I'm reminded I AM changing because God's in me, gently nudging me to do what's right. I just have to trust his Spirit to help me follow through.

Now, go be Great!

Running Out Of Gas...

So a girlfriend and I went out for a late lunch yesterday. We were driving separately and she called me as we passed a gas station and asked did I want to stop and grab some gas. Especially since everyone's panicking over gas stations running out of gas.

Wouldn't you know – where we stopped had that red plastic over the pump indicating they had NO GAS. I wasn't surprised, and pulled out and proceeded to go to our lunch spot. I was completely unbothered. Maybe because I had a little more than a quarter tank of gas or maybe because I REALLY WASN'T BOTHERED.

Not panic-strickened. My devotion reminded me why.

Phillipians 4:5 says "Don't fret or worry. Instead of worrying pray…let God know your concerns. He'll bring everything together for good."

I'm reminded, not to worry about being short on gas, instead fill up with faith and trusting in God.

Now, go be Great!

I Can't Find Gas

When I arrived back from vacation last night, it was 'back to reality'. And part of the 'reality' was FIND SOME GAS. It was dark, I was tired and decided "I'm just NOT going to worry about this now. I'll handle in the morning."

In the morning, I did find gas. And I thought – Janine, that's how you should handle all of your worries. It said so in my devotion,

Matthew 6:33. "Seek first His kingdom and His righteousness, and all these things will be given to you. Therefore do not worry about tomorrow, tomorrow will worry about itself…."

So when I was trying to find my gas last night and decided NOT TO WORRY, there was a peace in that. Knowing if I STAY CLOSE TO GOD, instead of the worry…HE WILL COMFORT ME. HE WILL GIVE ME PEACE. I'm reminded there's no room for worry when there's GOD.

Now, go be Great!

Do I Know How To Fight?

I was catching up on the phone with my cousin the other night and I was explaining how I think I'm doing better about having disagreements with my brother. We don't always agree on how to help my niece – his daughter.

When we both get fired up, we say things we don't really mean. And honestly, nothing really gets accomplished except for flared tempers. But this time, I was happy to tell my cousin my brother & I had a great talk without using hurtful words and got some resolve.

When I read my devotion today, it reiterated what I learned.

Colossians 3:8 "…rid yourself of all such things as these –anger, rage, malice, slander, and filthy language from your lips."

The bible actually tells you how to argue. I'm NOT supposed to focus on the blame, but focus on fixing the problem. I'm reminded to fight fair. That's what God wants me to do.

Now, go be Great!

The Need To Unsubscribe

I spent a good part of my evening last night UNSUBSCRIBING to all these emails I'd been getting. I couldn't figure out where they came from. I never subscribed to them!

They were emails on medications I'd never heard of, global technology, merger agreements from Canada. It was crazy! I know I trashed over 250 of those emails. Like in trash where it says SELECT ALL? I did. PERMANENTLY DELETED them.

Then I thought wouldn't that be great if I could do the same thing in life? GET RID of those things like bad habits, attitude and even negative people. But when I read my devotion, God says I can. He gives me free will.

Galatians 5:13 says "God has called you to a free life." But it also says, "don't use this freedom to do whatever you want. Instead, use it to love & serve others."

I'm reminded I CAN BE FREE to unsubscribe to the clutter and trash in my life. But, I can also be free to CHOOSE God & let His spirit lead me.

Now, go be Great!

When The Bridge Is Steep

I was reminiscing about my vacation in Savannah, GA. I was driving with my girlfriend and our moms when we had to cross this huge bridge. I'll have to admit, it was scary and steep. It looked like a rollercoaster, but we had to cross it to get to our Airbnb.

Anyway, as we began to cross – I think my girlfriend had a panic attack. Meanwhile, I was waiting for her to give me directions from her phone so I'd know whether to turn right or left once we crossed the bridge. She couldn't so I looked at my phone.

That sent my girlfriend into a tizzy – she was screaming as we continued to cross the bridge. I stayed calm. And told her to "calm down. I got this." And I did. We crossed the bridge successfully. I later thought that's how I sometimes act when I can't control a situation, think the worst like my girlfriend & panic. And all the while GOD is saying "Calm down. I got this." And He does. I'm reminded, when I'm met with a challenge (even crossing what looks to be an uncrossable bridge), to 'calm down' and know God is there. Airbnb.

Now, go be Great!

She Made A God-Move

I'm watching a movie yesterday and this father was fussing at this little girl who was like 11 or 12 years old. The father was enraged and said to the little girl "For once, why can't you just be a kid!" You can tell the WAY he said it really cut deep. Man, it hurt ME!

The little girl just stood there staring at him, not saying anything. But you could see the hurt on her face. Then, she did something I couldn't believe! She went over and hugged him really hard and told him "It's okay, dad! I know you didn't mean it." I got emotional.

I was thinking – now that's turning the other cheek! Did she really forgive him like that?? The dad turned around and apologized to her. My devotion today

Matthew 6:14 & 15 "You can't get forgiveness from God without also forgiving others."

What that little girl did was a God move. I'm reminded, to do my part when angry & hurt. Like the little girl, make a God move. Do it His way. Forgive.

Now, go be Great!

Finding Contentment

I'm doing a home improvement project. So, I recently went over a list – in my head & on paper -- of things I've gotten for my home and things I need to get. Everything from new fixtures, carpet, sofa and even accent pillows.

Anyway, thankfully a lot of those things I have gotten, but I still realize there a few other items I need to make my home improvement project complete. But, do I?

When I read my devotion this morning – it shook me.

1st Timothy 6:6-10 says "But godliness with contentment is a great gain."

It says we didn't bring anything into the world and we won't take anything out of it. And not to fall into the trap of wanting to be rich – with money or things. The love of money is the root of all evil. And lastly, I have everything I need IN GOD and nothing else. So, I'm reminded to redo my list. To have true riches and true contentment, put God first.

Now, go be Great!

Getting To Know Him

So there's this guy I like - sort of – and he likes me – sort of. I say 'sort of' because we both agreed to hang out and get to know each other, but our schedules haven't allowed it. So far, we've only connected once.

In being honest with myself, I thought "Janine, clearly this is not a priority for you right now." Like, how do you really get to know someone by only seeing him in your spare time? My devotion today posed the same question with God. How do you REALLY get to know God Janine, in your spare time?

The answer, I realized is – I DON'T. I read

Philippians 3:8 when Paul says "Everything else is worthless when compared with the value of knowing Jesus Christ."

Paul discarded everything else as garbage, so he could gain Christ. I had to ask myself "Am I treating God like this guy I like & trying to get close to know Him in my spare time?" I'm reminded I can get as close to God as I CHOOSE to. I just need to CHOOSE GOD FIRST -- EVERYDAY.

Now, go be Great!

Forgetting The Pain

A friend and I were venting on the phone, just about life, work, family and just how uncomfortable things can get sometimes. I heard her say "I'm just ready for this period to be over!" I told her, "It will be. God can make it as if it never happened."

I actually compared our discomfort to having a baby. I've never been pregnant, but find it amazing how women go through the discomfort sometimes of being pregnant and then having the baby, the excruciating pain! But, then after they have the baby, they DON'T REMEMBER the pain. My mom told me once "You just forget it. As if it never happened. And you enjoy the beauty of the baby."

I thought about that –'forgetting the pain' must be a gift from God. Then I thought I can apply this to my everyday life. I'll have pain, it's part of the process. But, know God will deliver me from it. He can wipe away the pain as if it never happened, like having a baby. I'm reminded God can help me 'forget the pain' & make room for the beauty of His blessings.

Now, go be Great!

Am I A Guest User?

I opened my laptop like I've done so many times, but really just realized I could choose to be a guest user and not as myself. I clicked it just to see and saw it didn't have any of the programs or icons I was accustomed to on my laptop. It was like I was operating on someone else's computer; a stranger's laptop.

I did not see MY documents, or MY folders or MY photos. Under my name, I see those things. I can relate and be confident I can get my work done. Quite honestly, seeing what I knew made me feel safe.

I thought about that's how it is with God. NOT choosing Him, I feel lost. Kind of like me operating as a guest on my computer. I don't want to be a guest with God. I want to be familiar with Him; comfortable with Him. And He wants me to be, too. I'm reminded I don't have to CHOOSE to operate as a guest with God. Because God is HOME and I choose Him - period.

Now, go be Great!

When To Stick With What I Know

My girlfriend called me while she was buying another laptop. I said – again??!! She just bought one right before the pandemic, because hers was done!

I tried to persuade her then to switch up and perhaps go with a MAC like me especially since she's bought two new computers in the last six years. Needless to say, she finally bought a MAC. But now, she's searching for another computer?? I asked her what happened.

She said, "I can't do it, lady. That MAC is too complicated & stressful. I'm gonna stick with what I know." I sighed and thought how many times have I done that too. Stress & give up. My devotion today

Psalm 46:10 says "Let go of your concerns! Then you will know that I am God. I rule the nations & the earth."

I thought I get stressed (in life) because I'm in conflict with God – and I never win the fight. I just get tired like my friend. Her dilemma reminded me, I'm NOT in control. God is – and He can make things right when I surrender to Him. Surrendering to Him gives me peace.

Now, go be Great!

I Focused On The Unknown

A friend and I were chatting about the future and retirement. And I have to be honest – I think we worked ourselves up to a frenzy. We both started asking all these questions like will we have enough money to retire, and after we retire? Where will we live, will we be in a Golden Girls house? Will we be married by then? The questions went on…

And once I started really thinking about it, it was a little scary, the unknown. Until I settled down and read my devotion.

Mark 11:22 put it quite simply. "Have faith in God."

And verse 24 – "Whatever you ask for in prayer, BELIEVE that you have received it and it will be yours."

I told myself – "It's not complicated, Janine." God says it's simple and not to get caught in the unknown of the future. Instead, I'll stay focused on what I DO KNOW and what God says – PRAY AND BELIEVE.

Now, go be Great!

Missing The Moment

I was smiling last night as I watched Alyssa lead an IG Live for the nonprofit I started called Girl Talk. I had actually imagined this and prayed for someone who'd share the same passion as I have had for Girl Talk for some time now.

That it would eventually happen. And right before my eyes – it was HAPPENING, IN REAL TIME! I took in that moment longer today as I had my devotion. And I thought 'Yes, that thing you prayed for Janine, it IS HAPPENING! Right Now!" It's not 'down the road.'

Then I thought how many times have I missed that MOMENT when I prayed for something and the moment happens, but I miss it because I'm caught up in the busyness of everyday life, stress or what I thought it should look like. But, today I didn't miss it. I could see God working it out. Like he said in

1st Thessalonians 5:24 "The One who called you is completely dependable. If He said it, He'll do it."

So, thank you God – for helping me NOT miss the MOMENT.

Now, go be Great!

No Matter The Storm

I was looking out on my balcony – it was cloudy & gloomy. And I saw two birds fluttering around and landed on my balcony. I was thinking these birds seem so happy and gleeful and thought "Don't they know it's about to storm? They better seek shelter.

I'm not certain if they did or not, but I later thought I want to be like those birds – in life.

Though at times, things seem gloomy, or not going my way, I still want to be able to celebrate and be happy. And God says that's how I should be, too.

In my devotion today,

Habakkuk (Huh-BACK-kuk) 3:17 & 18 "Even though the fig trees have no blossoms, no grapes on the vine, fields are empty & barren…I will rejoice in the Lord."

I'm reminded, despite any storm, like those birds, I'll continue to fly. I'll to continue to praise Him.

Now, go be Great!

I've Got To Apply

On the phone with my cousin recapping our day. We ended up having a bible study, relating our day to the word, encouraging each other and so on.

Towards the end of our talk, we both agreed we know what to do and who to turn to in times of difficulty, confusion and frustration. We know God is the only one who can fix all of that!

But, we also both realized while we KNOW what to do, we don't always DO IT. In fact, I said we need to switch up our prayer and ask God to help us APPLY what we know. I thought, it's like knowing you need to get healthy and workout but never workout. In my devotion

Ephesians 6:13 says "Be prepared. You're up against far more than YOU can handle…".

I'm reminded KNOWING who to turn to and KNOWING God's word are crucial…but APPLYING God's word is LIFE-CHANGING.

Now, go be Great!

I Got Signed Out

I was on my phone paying a few bills the other day. I inadvertently left open my bank account page because I received the message, 'we are signing you out, due to inactivity.' Obviously, a safety precaution.

As I read my devotion today, I thought about that message and thought sometimes in life when things are challenging, when I'm going through…it can feel like God isn't there, like He's signed out. But that's not true.

Psalm 46:1 says "God is our refuge and strength, a very present help in trouble."

That's when God IS there – when I'm broken or lost. I'm reminded, unlike the bank message that told me it was signing me out because I wasn't active…God never signs out on me. He's ALWAYS PRESENT, even when it doesn't feel like it. I'm encouraged – to stay ACTIVE with God, Janine. Afterall, He's ALWAYS with me.

Now, go be Great!

The Storm I Almost Missed

I worked late yesterday…I was really focused on getting some work completed before I head out on vacation. When I finally finished and was leaving the building, I realized there had been a whole storm that came through the area. Some debris had been scattered and the ground was soaked.

In fact, it was still storming. I had practically missed it. I had no idea all that was happening outside. I had been so caught up in my work.

That hit me today when I had my devotion. Janine, that's how God wants you to be with Him. So caught up in Him, so focused on Him that I don't pay attention to life's turbulence – worry, doubt, fear.

Proverbs 1:7 says "Start with God."

I'm reminded when I put God FIRST and put my focus and energy on Him instead of my troubles, my storms LOSE their power.

Now, go be Great!

Enjoying The Now

I saw a friend's post the other day. It was HER inspirational moment and through it, I got inspired. She talked about going through seasons. She's expecting her baby boy any day now and said she really wanted this season to be over. She's over being pregnant.

But then she went on to say…she wasn't going to rush it. That she realized this moment was a part of this season and that she'd enjoy it. I thought about that today during my devotion that reminded me not to be anxious – like my friend said.

In fact, Philippians 4: 6 says just that "Do not be anxious about anything."

And my friend said she's going to enjoy this season. My friend's inspiration was a great inspiration and reminder for me: NOT to worry about tomorrow. Be content in the now. And know I don't have to crave for the next season. God is enough NOW.

Now, go be Great!

Chasing Him Down

Chatting with a friend recently and I complimented him on his business. He is really thriving despite the pandemic. I let him know how proud of him I was. He thanked me and explained his process.

He said before now, he'd really been struggling. That on the outside he probably seemed okay, but on the inside he was stressed. But then he said something that struck me. He said, Janine I chased God down. He told me he'd never prayed that hard before. Then things started happening.

I thought… I don't think I've been chasing God down. And that's what God desires. He wants me to SEEK HIM like my friend did, with everything that's in me. My devotion today

Matthew 6:33 "Seek first his kingdom & his righteousness and all these things will be given to you."

My friend chased God down. God says seek Him. I'm reminded to just let go, Janine and SEEK GOD.

Now, go be Great!

No More Sound

Do you ever crave quiet? I was driving home the other day with NO SOUND. Then I got home and again – NO SOUND. Meaning… no tv, no Pandora, no google voice, no Alexa, no Siri – nothing.

Probably like you, I'd been around sound all day. Now, I don't take hearing for granted, but sometimes I'm okay with NO SOUND. After reading my devotion today, I think that's an answer to a prayer I've had – to hear from God and receive His wisdom.

Psalm 46:10 says "Be still and know that I am God!"

My devotion said I don't hear God because I have too many other things cluttering my mind (work, bills, relationships). My devotion said it plain – Janine, to hear God, you gotta get near God and sometimes that means sit down and shut up.

Now, go be Great!

When The Day Is Cloudy...

While I was on vacation, it stormed one day. I mean thundering, lightning. And I was starting to think 'Oh, boy! Not a good vacation day! We're gonna have to be confined to being inside.' The rain was actually beginning to change my attitude about the day.

But reading my devotion John 15: 1-9 helped me change my thinking. It talks about my being the grapevine and God being the gardener and how I can't produce anything unless God is in me. In other words, as a vine I cannot produce fruit unless I'm connected to God - period.

So I thought when God is in me, it doesn't matter what's happening on the outside – even if it's a rainy day on my vacation or circumstances in my life look gloomy --- the key is having Christ, God, living in me. I'm reminded no matter what, God is my source for contentment, confidence, calm and I'll choose to draw from Him.

Now, go be Great!

When The Limb Is Dead

I was watering my plants the other day. The plant that's inside is one I've had for years. It's been growing all over the place, I've never really trimmed it – fearful I would somehow stunt its growth.

But, it was this one limb I could not ignore because it was completely brown & dry. Clearly, it was dead, but the other limbs on the plant were a vibrant, shiny green. I was hesitant, but I just snapped that brown, dead limb off. I thought 'my whole plants gonna die now.'

But some weeks later, it did just the opposite. It continued to grow & flourish. And I thought God doesn't want me holding on to what's old like that dead limb. He says in

Isaiah 43 - verses 18 & 19, "Forget the former things. He's about to do something brand new!"

I'm reminded, like my plant God wants me to flourish. And I'll trust Him to make a NEW way.

Now, go be Great!

Staying In The Race

I woke up this morning feeling a little blah. Then I saw more headlines about this track star named Sha'Carri Richardson who if you watched the Olympic trials was called one of the fastest women in the world. She finished a 100 meters in 10.64 seconds and will represent US in the Olympics Track & Field.

And in the midst of celebrating her win, she told reporters her biological mom died the previous week. I'm thinking what? But that didn't stop her from running the race. In spite of…Sha'Carri said "I'm still here."

I'm thinking – INCREDIBLE. I'm still here, too. Even though I woke up this morning feeling 'blah.' I'm still here. My devotion for today:

Psalm 27:14. "I'll see God's goodness in the earth. Stay with God. Take heart. Don't quit. Stay with God."

I'm reminded, don't let a blah day stop you Janine. Like Sha'Carri – finish the race. And stay with God.

Now, go be Great!

I Gave Up My Bag

While traveling by air a few weeks ago, I of course, checked one bag. I don't know about you, but once I've checked my bag and received my boarding pass - a sigh of relief comes over me. I think – whew – almost done.

Anyway, after getting on the plane I started thinking about the entire flying process and my luggage. And thought – I'm really so trusting. I didn't think twice about American Airlines getting my bag where it needed to be. The last I saw of it, it was on a conveyer belt, disappearing in a dark hole.

Did I worry? No, not at all. I just gave up my luggage – just like that. Trusting it'll get to the same place I'm going. When I had my devotion today, I thought that's the same kind of trust I need to have in God.

Isaiah 12:2 "God is my salvation. I will trust & not be afraid. The Lord is my strength."

I'm reminded, if I can so easily give up my luggage to the airline, certainly I can hand over my other baggage -- anxiety, fear, doubt -- to God. I will TRUST GOD.

Now, go be Great!

They Answered Before I Called

I didn't receive a package I had ordered online. So I activated the retailers chat feature to try and get answers. I explained. The rep said they would follow up. Later that same day I decided to also just call the retailer to make sure they were going to investigate.

Before I could even call, I got an email alerting me my package would be replaced and what date I should expect it. I have to admit I was a bit shocked. I didn't even get to call to follow up. They were on it!

That's why when I read my devotion today it made so much sense because that's how God operates.

Isaiah 65:24 says "Before they call I will answer; while they are still speaking I will hear."

God says that while I'm praying, He's answering. And I needed that because sometimes I forget. But, just like the retailer – God can answer with a quickness. I'll keep the faith and thank Him in advance.

Now, go be Great!

What Am I Waiting For?

I was clearing out my inbox this morning and saw a 'reminder' email from Bath & Body Works. I had some items remaining in a cart, so they were reminding me about them. Amazing how they do that.

But, it was something different in how I saw the message. The reminder said "You still have good stuff in your shopping bag. What are you waiting for?" The WHAT ARE YOU WAITING FOR glared out to me. What AM I waiting for?

I had just decided to join a professional group that could potentially generate another revenue stream, but I hadn't finished my profile. I have two standout interviewees for my podcast on hold – they were waiting for me to send dates. I felt God was talking to me in that reminder email. Just like in life 'What are you waiting for Janine? God still has good stuff in your shopping bag (planted in me).' I hear God in my Bath & Body reminder message. What are you waiting for? He's saying ACTIVATE Him now. Cast out the fear & believe.

Now, go be Great!

When The Writing Isn't On The Wall

I keep various scriptures or inspirational quotes around me in my home. There's one that I've been missing though. It's a framed piece that says "No weapons formed against me shall prosper." The frame is being repaired, so I had to take it down.

I've needed that framed scripture… because sometimes I feel defeated and like I'm under attack by the enemy. For example, I'm not getting out my video inspirations like I used to; thinking negatively.

But what I realized this morning is just because that framed scripture isn't on my wall, doesn't mean the scripture is missing, or that it doesn't stand true. My devotion today - - John 11 when Jesus let Lazarus die, then brought him back to life & in verse 25 told his sister that,

"I am the Resurrection and Life. And if you believe in me; you will live."

I'm reminded even though I can feel under attack, the enemy is NO weapon against God. And I don't need a frame on the wall to believe that. God is with me, no matter what.

Now, go be Great!

Getting My Car Washed Blessed Me

My cousin and I were on the phone talking about family stuff. We were both trying to help our neice "find her way." We both were asking, "Is she hearing us?"

Anyway, I was thinking about new ways to help my niece as I went through the car wash the other day. As the car wash process started – I did the usual. Put the car in neutral, took my foot off the pedal; I even turned off the music.

I forgot how relaxing going through the car wash was. No talking, no decision making, no stress, just glided through the car wash. I was just being. And it hit me –

Janine, this is how God wants you to be when you start to try and fix things. Take your hand off the wheel and your foot off the pedal. Let God guide you…like going through the car wash. I'm reminded I can avoid the exhaustion from trying to fix things, when I let God lead. Let God lead.

Now, go be Great!

Am I Dehydrated?

I was reading an article the other day on the importance of staying hydrated. And how most of us don't get enough water. The article said generally speaking women should drink at least 11 ½ cups and men 15 ½ cups of water a day.

Then the article talked about the benefits of water: helps regulate your body temperature, flushes out bacteria, even helps with your mood and memory, anxiety and fatigue. We NEED water to survive. And I thought am I getting enough?

And then I thought sometimes I think I'm dehydrated – spiritually. If I'm being honest, sometimes I don't get enough God in my day. I sometimes skip talking with Him because of time. But, I thought just like water, He IS an essential part of my well-being – helping to REGULATE me, FLUSHING OUT what I don't need, HELPING relieve my anxiety. I'm reminded, NOT to get dehydrated of God. I will continue to THIRST for Him like water, I NEED God EVERYDAY.

Now, go be Great!

I Think Too Much

Talking with a girlfriend about faith. She said she'd just heard a speaker talk on that very thing. What he said, I thought, was profound. He said if you're an overthinker, or always analyze, there's no room for faith for those kinds of people.

She went on to say he explained when you over think or analyze, you're really trying to control and that doesn't align with faith or God. He said with God – faith is simple. You pray, you believe, you let go. That's it. He said we complicate faith by overthinking.

And I just did – in thinking about my career, my family, the future. The speaker said that's not our job to figure out how. Hearing her say that made perfect sense and served as a great reminder when I read

Psalm 56:11. "In God have I put my trust. I will not be afraid."

So, I will trust God and let go.

Now, go be Great!

When The Ride Is Bumpy

I flew home from my vacation yesterday and the weather was dreary. I was in Florida where most people were preparing for Hurricane Elsa to make impact. I was glad our flight wasn't delayed. But, during the flight it was bumpy. The plane was dipping and diving a bit. It was cloudy & gray.

I was thinking 'Is this gonna be the remainder of the ride.' But it wasn't. In the next 10 minutes…as we ascended, it looked like a whole new sky. It was bright, clear, no rain. It was as if the storm just vanished. I thought – the pilot knew to fly ABOVE the storm & take us out of harm's way.

Then I thought – that's how God does, when I let Him. While on that plane, I had no control. I couldn't fly it. I HAD to relinquish my control. EXACTLY how I need to do in life. And in my devotion

Matthew 16:24, God says it. "Anyone who intends to come with me has to let me lead. You're not in the driver's seat. I am."

I'm reminded again, when I let God lead – the sky opens up just like on my flight. Cloudy skies become clear; the bumps in my life smooth out. Let God lead, Janine.

Now, go be Great!

I Was At The Edge Of The Pool

While on vacation, my cousin and I got into the pool. We were both just playing around with floating. But we were holding on to the edge of the pool.

Which obviously doesn't work well. We both knew in order to float we had to be free from the EDGE of the pool. We knew we had to let go to have our bodies FREE and be completely surrounded by water.

We continued to play around. But later, I thought about the act of floating. To float – requires you to be completely RELAXED, FREE from ANXIETY & TENSION. I thought that's just like having God work in my life. I can't hang on to the edge of the pool. I have to let go and let God guide my life. Like floating, I have to free myself from anxiety, tension, & rest on the surface of the water. I'm reminded, to float I can't hang on to the edge of the pool. Just like with God, I have to TRUST, let go, and REST on Him.

Now, go be Great!

I Only Wanted To Find A Tank Top

Have you ever had a situation that was supposed to be so simple, but it turns into a 'thing'? For example, I ordered a tank top. A simple thing, right? It was on back order – until like late August.

Tried another retailer. They had tanks, but only razorback tanks. I didn't want that. Tried a third retailer, they are out of stock!! This was supposed to be a simple task, not a major project! WHY?

When I read my devotion today, I thought about my situation – having to 'go through' just to get a tank top. My devotion said I need to consider the source of any adversity. Life's adversities.

Isaiah 45:5-10 says it. God forms the light and creates darkness; makes harmonies & creates discord.

And we are NOT to fight HIM. I'm reminded instead of focusing on the hardship, focus on God & His faithfulness. He's using it for His purpose and to make me better.

Now, go be Great!

Removing The Doubt

I was on the phone with a girlfriend who was telling me about her upcoming career plans. She'd set some goals and laid out deadlines to meet them, too. In fact, we both shared our next moves and were excited about it. Some may even think over zealous.

After ending our call, I replayed our conversation in my head and realized nowhere in our talk did either one of us doubt our plans. We spoke with confidence, as if it had already happened.

When I read my devotion today, I thought 'Yes, Janine that's what God wants you to do.' In Mark 9:23, Jesus responded to a father who wanted to know if Jesus could remove a demon from his son's body. Jesus said, "If? There are no 'if's' among believers. Anything can happen." I'm reminded, my girlfriend and I weren't being cocky when talking about our next plans, we were being BELIEVERS because God CAN DO anything.

Now, go be Great!

The Nudge

My cousin and I were talking as we often do. On this particular occasion, she suggested I do something quite frankly, I just didn't agree with. When she repeated it and I did nothing – she asked 'Did you hear me?' I said, 'Yes, I hear you – I just don't want to do it.'

I thought about my response later and thought – I do do that sometimes with God. That He, the Spirit may be nudging me to do something that's uncomfortable for me – like writing my book, continuing to work out. And I know it's Him nudging me. But, I don't always do it.

In my devotion –

James 1:22-25 – talks about "being DOERS of the word and NOT HEARERS only."

I realized God is always whispering plans in my ears even when I don't feel comfortable doing it. I'm reminded when I hear God nudge me to do the uncomfortable or scary thing, I need to let my guard down, step out and do it. Nothing is too big or scary for Him.

Now, go be Great!

When You're Being Boring

I had a strong desire to sit on my balcony yesterday – wasn't too hot, nice breeze. I was just chill-laxing. In fact, I was taking a friends advice who said sometimes you just need to SLOW DOWN, so I was.

Another friend called. He asked what I was doing. I told him – chilling on the balcony. He asked did I have a drink, too. I said yes, water. He said, that's boring. I said I'll take boring.

Because boring is giving me peace. Boring is giving me clarity. Boring is giving me calm. Boring is giving me ME time with God. So, yes, I'll take boring. I'm reminded having a GOOD life isn't always hype and being lit. The best life is paying attention to God's nudge to SLOW DOWN and yes, to even be BORING.

Now, go be Great!

When You're Not Welcomed

The other day a couple of my neighbors were in the hallway as I got off the elevator. I stopped to chat a bit and then as I headed into my unit, I invited them to stop in for a bit. It was rather impromptu. They accepted. We chatted briefly & then they left.

Before they left, I invited them to come back when we all had more time. They said "cool". I thought later about our interaction. And thought it was easy to welcome them into my home – they were cool; I know them. They are my neighbors.

I thought just as easy as I welcomed people I knew, I sometimes welcome feelings that don't belong, like fear and anxiety. In my devotion, God says in John 14: 26 & 27…that He gives me peace. And that I shouldn't let my heart be troubled or afraid. I'm reminded while I welcomed neighbors into my home, I NEED to close the door to doubt, fear, anxiety.. They are NOT WELCOMED here. But God is. AND I WILL WELCOME & OPEN THE DOOR TO HIM.

Now, go be Great!

My Activity Plan

I got an email from Google, reminding me what will happen if my account becomes inactive for two months. I actually set it up after Google prompted me. I was thinking 'there is NO WAY, I'm NOT going to be active on Google or two months!"

Anyway, my plan is after two months of inactivity – Google will try to contact me through three different emails. After three months they'll notify a friend…then finally delete my account.

I was shaking my head as I reviewed Google's plan – and thought they have a plan for EVERYTHING. Their plan for MY INACTIVITY made me think about MY plan of ACTIVITY with God. I talk to him everyday! But, when I'm NOT ACTIVE with HIM, I DO feel lost and out of the loop. Like NOT being ACTIVE on Google for two months. Except, God doesn't DELETE me if I'm inactive. Instead

Psalm 46:1 says "He's my refuge and strength and present when I'm in trouble."

I'm reminded I don't NEED an ACTIVITY plan with God, I just need to know God is always there & waiting for me.

Now, go be Great!

When You're Stuck In Traffic

I took an Uber a few days ago. We had to get on I-77 and of course traffic was tight. We'd been at a crawl for about a minute, when the driver asked me if I knew of a faster route. Though we were only cruising, I told her to just stick it out.

I explained it had happened to me earlier. When I first got on the interstate, traffic was tight, bottle-necked. But then after a few minutes, it opened up. And just as I was saying that, traffic loosened and lanes opened up.

When I had my devotion today, I recalled that Uber ride in traffic. God was speaking to me. I could hear Him saying just as I advised the Uber driver to "just stick it out". Hang on a little longer, Janine. Though it seems like I'm stuck, God's gonna open it up like the lanes on I-77 and I'll MOVE! I'm reminded in

Jeremiah 29:11 "God has a plan for me..."

So, Trust God and His plan.

Now, go be Great!

Trapped Inside

Over the weekend, I was with my family in Greensboro. Me, my mom and cousin went out to eat, but got trapped inside the restaurant.

I say trapped, because it started raining so hard, like a torrential rainstorm. We decided to wait it out inside the restaurant. After about 10 minutes more of conversation, we looked out and the sun was beginning to shine. No rain – anywhere. It just completely stopped. No lightning, no sprinkling, no nothing. The rain had ceased – just like that.

It's been doing that throughout the last few days – rain, rain, rain – then nothing. And I thought, that's a lot like life, too. I have those moments of despair, storms in life – an off day, feeling discouraged. But, God. He can wipe it all away. Just as quickly as those storms rose and disappeared, God can bring the sunshine in my life. There will be thunderstorms in life, but I'm reminded go to God, it's He who can stop the rain.

Now, go be Great!

When The Hill Is Steep

I was watching a movie last night where a couple was escaping wildfires in California. The husband knew of a path they could walk alongside the mountain that would lead them to safety. The wife resisted at first, but went.

They reached a cliff that they would have to descend and it was nothing but rock. It was their only way out. The wife said, "There is NO WAY I can climb down this steep hill of rock!" She was scared to death…Anyway, the husband went first, coached her & she made it!

Reading my devotion today – I could totally relate to the wife's fear and doubt. Sometimes in life, I'm thinking 'where is this money gonna come from?' 'How will I ever get THIS JOB?' My faith wavers like the Israelites in Deuteronomy 1:26-28, doubting what God had already promised them. They chose, like me sometimes to listen to the wrong voices; they chose to rely on human reasoning instead of knowing the greatness of God; and they chose their feelings of fear over faith. I'm reminded, no matter the challenge CHOOSE to courageously TRUST GOD. Like the woman in the movie climbing down a hill of rock, there are blessings on the other side. GOD WILL DO WHAT HE SAYS. TRUST HIM.

Now, go be Great!

What Am I Seeing?

I went with my mom recently to the eye doctor. It was a routine check as she had cateract surgery on her eyes a while back. Anyway, she had a pretty good report. The doctor, to my surprise, says she has 20/20 vision in BOTH EYES. I said 'Okay, Mama at 81.' Technically, she can see better than me??!!

I thought about my vision when I read my devotion today.

1st Samuel 16: verse 7 says what God told Samuel. "Don't judge by his appearance or height for I have rejected him. God doesn't SEE how WE see. He looks at the heart."

And I thought God can see PAST what WE see. And there are several examples of that in the Bible. John 4:1-42 when he met the woman at the well in Samaria. He didn't just see a prostitute, He saw someone broken & thirsty for life. I thought I want to SEE like God. He's not judgmental, find fault or gets jealous. I'm reminded, to begin to SEE like God. I need to fix MY EYES – on Him & His Word.

Now, go be Great!

The Urge

You know when you have a tugging in your heart, that's really God urging you to do what He's asked you to do. Even if it's uncomfortable or you flat out just don't want to do it.

I get like that sometimes. And to be honest, it's been that way with my inspirational moments on VIDEO. God wants me to do it, to teach people who may not other wise hear me deliver it on the radio. But, why haven't I done it? Lazy. Off course. I've gotten off track. But yet I still want God to bless me in this way or the other.

When I woke up this morning – I heard the horn of what sounded like a train. Which I rarely hear – being uptown. I believe it was a tug from God – nudging ME to get back on track. And only He can help me do that. So I started praying. "God move me to get back on track. Move me to complete your assignment." I was reminded the best way to get back on track, is to go to the master conductor. God will guide me.

Now, go be Great!

I Can Be Sometimey

I was on the phone with a friend recently. We hadn't talked in over a month, which is pretty unusual for us. Normally, we try to talk at least once a week. I was honest with her, saying I don't like our inconsistency.

I teased her saying, we're on-again off-again friends. We both laughed and agreed we CAN BE "SOMETIMEY". I thought about that & realized I'm that way at times with God.

Sometimes I pray, sometimes I don't. After reading my devotion, I'm so glad God isn't that way with me. He's NOT "sometimey." I can't imagine that sometimes, he'll forgive me; sometimes, he won't. Sometimes he listens to me, sometimes he doesn't.

Hebrews 13:8 says, "For Jesus doesn't change — yesterday, today, tomorrow. He's always totally himself."

I thought, Janine you need to be more like Jesus in your walk WITH HIM. No on-again, off-again with God. He's there all the time, the same. My prayer: God help me to be less sometimey & and more consistent like YOU.

Now, go be Great!

I Never See My Footprints

I went walking the other morning after it had rained earlier. So I noticed several footprints along my route – obviously where others had been before me.

Some of the footprints were large, some small. I even noticed some paw prints from what I assumed was a dog. Then I thought 'Janine, you're leaving footprints, too you know.' But when I really thought about it, I never see my footprints, because I never look back.

After reading my devotion today, that's how God wants me to be.

Philippians 3:14-17 - 'Forgetting what is behind and straining toward what is ahead; keeping my eye on the goal where God is.'

It even says keep people around you who are running the same course – who are moving towards God. I thought my never seeing my footprints is a good thing. I'm reminded to stay on track with God on my mind and never turn back.

Now, go be Great!

I'm Ready To Fly

My bestie hit me up last night chuckling at a text I sent her. It was a link to get her TSA PreCheck appointment. I already have mine. Because we both said we want to do more traveling so I'm getting ready and don't want to be in long lines waiting.

She says she chuckled because I'm already acting as if we have tickets purchased and rooms booked. I said "Of course." I told her, "I'm doing what God says." Pray for what you want and BELIEVE you'll get it.

When I read my devotion further today – it was in

> *Mark 11:24 that Jesus said "Whatever you desire, PRAY and BELIEVE you'll receive."*

In fact, Jesus urged the disciples to pray for absolutely EVERYTHING – small to large (like my international travel) as they embrace the God-life and get God's everything. But He also says it's not all ASKING. I gotta forgive, too. I'm reminded, God wants to GIVE me the desires of my heart. So, I'll ASK, I'll BELIEVE & WATCH GOD WORK.

Now, go be Great!

I Lost $100

I lost $100 a few weeks ago – to a client who agreed to pay, but didn't. Even though I did the work, they didn't pay. Of course, I wasn't happy initially. In fact, I was ticked off and wanted to continue to state my case and fight it.

But then, I just stopped and prayed and remembered – God's got this, Janine. Let it go. I kept thinking – I did the right thing, God's going to fix it. I don't know how…but He will fix it. And He did. In the last month, I started getting all these new opportunities and gigs. Even an agency from LA called with work for me.

And when I had my devotion this morning…I started thinking about all these NEW opportunities that far surpass that $100 I thought I'd lost. In Joel 2:25 God promises to restore what was lost and cause increase to come. I'm reminded, no matter how long the wait (for whatever it is), God will fix it & bring reward, I just have to choose FAITH over EVERYTHING.

Now, go be Great!

Expect Greatness

I went to bed rather late last night – trying to get a project finished. As I was working, I was thinking – I GOTTA get this DONE! And I was thinking, but I wanna be sleep. Why am I up doing this?' You know how you count to see how many hours of sleep you'll be able to get? That was me.

Anyway, I decided to shut it down. But before I did, I ran across an IG video from Beyonce. And it really spoke to me. She said she'd been blessed to have 24 Grammy's, but that she LOST 46 times.

I thought about that. We always see the glory, the triumph…but seldom see the struggle to get there. You know, how you want to stop, and give up. Beyonce's message– she didn't give up. She didn't stop. God says the same.

Psalm 31:24 says "Be brave. Be strong. Don't give up. EXPECT God to get here soon."

I'm reminded, Janine, don't be afraid of 'the work'. Just keep God in it and EXPECT GREATNESS from Him.

Now, go be Great!

Get A Grip

I've been working to get a better grip on my healthy lifestyle. You know, getting in regular exercise, eating well again, staying away from junk food. I know as I get older, I have to work a little harder to maintain good health.

And as I had my devotion today, I thought I need to work a little harder to be spiritually healthy, too. Pastor Rick Warren says the Bible is my soul food. He explained I should FEED on the word of God to get all of His blessings. To do that, I should do 6 things:

HEAR God's word, READ His word, STUDY it, MEMORIZE it, MEDITATE on it and finally APPLY it.

And Acts 20:32 summed it up. "The message of his grace…is able to build you up & give you the blessings of God." I'm reminded, the same way I want to get a grip on a healthy lifestyle…I'll need to get a GRIP on God's word.

Now, go be Great!

Enduring The Pain

While getting my hair done yesterday, you know my hairstylist (Shout out to Derickus) dropped a jewel on me. I had noticed his latest tattoos. One completely covers one arm – I had never seen it before. Then another tattoo covered one of his legs.

I was amazed! He told me he had to be in the mood to get them. I asked what he meant.

He says you have to have your head in a certain space in order to endure the constant pain of a tattoo. He said some people just can't stand the pain & tap out.

All that talk about tattoos and enduring pain got me thinking about the struggle and discomfort I sometimes experience in life. At times, I don't think I can take it. That led me to my devotion today –

James 1:12 says "God blesses those who patiently endure testing and temptation."

In the end, God will reward them. I'm reminded life does have it's pain like getting a tattoo, but I don't have to run from it or tap out. I can endure because I've got God.

Now, go be Great!

It's The Little Things

You ever have one of those days or even moments when NOTHING is going the way you want? That was me the other day. I was finishing up a pretty big project on my laptop and the program I was working in stopped working. I lost the project.

I received a bill with a large charge I now have to dispute. And two warning lights popped up on my car dashboard. Finally, I just sat in my living room and sighed. While I was in my feelings, two birds flew on my balcony. The semed so at peace, just chirping and eating seeds.

Watching those birds forced me to take a beat and breathe and think. And I thought 'these birds' are God's work. They brought me peace and made me realize I should cherish the little things, like birds chirping on my balcony. My devotion said it, too.

First Thessalonians 5:18 "In EVERY THING give thanks, it's the will of God."

I'm reminded, in the midst of it all (whatever it is), I will cherish the little things, give thanks to God for them. And know He has more good things in store for me.

Now, go be Great!

I Won't Keep Him Waiting

A good girlfriend moved away recently. She and I used to talk at least every other day, but now we don't. And I miss that. Life happens, work, you get busy. But, I'll see her this weekend and I can't wait! We have so much to catch up on.

We haven't talked in a minute, so I'm excited. I want us to get back on our regular schedule of talking. During my devotion today, I realized that's probably how God feels if I go days and weeks without talking to Him. If I'm being honest, I have let an entire day go by without talking to God.

But Isaiah 30:18 says God doesn't punish me for not talking to Him. It says

"The Lord still waits for me to come to him so he can show me His love."

He is waiting. Just like me and my girlfriend who haven't talked in a while. God doesn't let LIFE get in the way. He IS LIFE & is available 24/7. I'm reminded – I won't leave God waiting. He's waiting on me.

Now, go be Great!

When There's No Sunshine

Usually the sunrise wakes me up in the morning – around 6 thirty-ish. But on this particular day that didn't happen. When I got up – there was no sun shining brightly which made me think it was still early. It wasn't – it was after 7am. Then I thought – 'Okay. It must be raining; it's gonna be gloomy & gray today.'

I looked out on my balcony, it wasn't raining, but was a little gray. So I settled back in bed to read. About 30 minutes went by – and lo' and behold, my whole bedroom had lit up. The sun was shining just as bright. There wasn't a cloud in the sky.

During my devotion, I could hear God talking to me in that moment. I heard 'no matter how gray, dark or gloomy things look Janine (in your life) – God CAN turn things around. He can set things right! My day started out what I saw as gray & gloomy, but God brought out the sunshine & gave me this testimony to remind me of HIS AWESOME POWER. He can change anything!

Now, go be Great!

What Am I Rushing For Again?

Do you ever feel tired AFTER you get to work or if you're home as you BEGIN work, you're already tired? That was me one day last week. In fact, I felt like I rushed through the whole day.

Of course, I had my devotion. Then my workout, then jumped on a Zoom call, then hurried to fix breakfast & snack, rushed in the shower, did makeup, hair, rushed to get into the car. Oh and I had to handle some business on the phone while driving. By the time I got to work, I was actually tired.

My devotion today said while Jesus was on earth, he was never in a hurry and God is NOT in a hurry now.

Ecclesiastes 3:1 message version says "There's an opportune time to do things, a right time for everything on earth…"

My devotion says learn to do things in God's rhythm and NOT the world's pace. I'm reminded there's no JOY in rushing. I'd rather have peace. I need to Trust God to give me the peace I need to LIVE life instead of rushing through it.

Now, go be Great!

What Brings Me Joy

I recently had an opportunity to do some acting work. At first I was excited then later, I got stressed. This opportunity would mean getting up before 9am any weekday morning. I wouldn't always know when.

The more I thought about it, the more stressed I got. I ended up turning it down. And I felt relieved. The next day, I was in my closet and saw one of my many post-it notes. They are words of empowerment and inspiration.

What stood out was a postcard I had written to myself. It was part of an exercise I did at a retreat in which we were asked to write ourselves a note reminding us of what's important to us. My note read "Remember, you DESERVE to be HAPPY. Do the things that bring you joy."

I could hear God in that note… nudging me that the uneasiness & angst I felt about that 'opportunity' was because it was NOT in alignment with His plan for me. I was reminded not every opportunity is God-sent. Learn to TRUST GOD to continue to guide my path.

Now, go be Great!

When It's The Little Stuff

I was reading an article recently about Kim Kardashian – I know, right. Go figure! But anyway, I really liked what she said. She was talking about her marriage to Kanye and admitted she had all the cars, clothes, and could go anywhere in the world she wanted. She had the big STUFF.

But Kim also said what she didn't have – in her marriage. She likes to workout, Kanye hates going to the gym. She likes holding hands and being affectionate, Kanye doesn't. Kim said I have all the BIG STUFF, but I want the LITTLE stuff.

During my devotion, I realized God cares about the little stuff.

In Luke 12:7 he says "even the very hairs on your head are all numbered."

And even our "little" worries in

Philippians 4:6 in which God says "do not be anxious about ANYTHING."

I'm reminded, God cares about me – period - even my little stuff.

Now, go be Great!

A Room With A View

My neighbor introduced me to something new at my own home! This may sound odd, but I had only been on my buildings rooftop once – even though I lived in my spot for years. I just never thought about it. But, the THE VIEW!

Oh, my God! I'm thinking when I'd see other places with a view, I'd be in awe! Saying in my head "Man, I'd love a view like that!" And lo and behold, I HAVE ONE and didn't even know it. Which is why when I had my devotion today – I just woke up and said thank you, God!

You DO hear me and you DO answer me. Sometimes I'm too distracted to even realize my blessings. My devotion said I should start each day – with gratitude, not with a list of requests. In fact,

James 1:17 says that "every good and perfect gift is from above, coming down from the heavenly Father & He doesn't change."

I'm reminded before I list what I DON'T have, remember God's goodness & wake up to worship!!

Now, go be Great!

What Am I Waking Up To?

I watched the news before heading to bed last night. Devastation everywhere. The coronavirus is surging again in the states; fires still blazing on the West coast. Hundreds dead after an earthquake in Haiti & thousands are fleeing Afghanistan after the Taliban took over the government.

Watching the news was exhausting and depressing & the wrong move before I went to bed. My rest wasn't so restful. When I had my devotion this morning, Pastor Rick Warren suggested before I end my day, remind myself of God's truth & end my day with a good word.

Like Matthew 6:13 part of the Lord's prayer "For Yours is the kingdom, the power & the glory forever. Amen."

Just reading that reminded me that God IS IN CONTROL, not politicians or other nations. And despite bad news, that's NOT how the story ends. With God, we win in the end. I'm reminded NOT to end my day with news, but end my day with God's truth playing in my head.

Now, go be Great!

Which Way Do I Go?

I had lunch with a friend a few days ago and we were catching up -- talking about her business and my ventures, too. Like good friends do, she offered me advice in some areas. Good advice, too. I took it in.

Later that evening, I thought about my friends advice – and advice I've gotten from others. And to be honest, thinking about all their advice, was a little overwhelming. Who do I listen to? What's next? What do I pray for? During my morning devotion, a simple question stung me. "What is guiding you?"

In reality, I have to make decisions ALL the time throughout the day – big & small. But my devotion reminded me I don't have to make decisions alone. God is there and ready to guide me. And God says it in

Psalm 32:8 "I will instruct thee and teach thee in the way which you should go."

So I'm reminded not to get overwhelmed or anxious when making decisions, go to God Janine and ask HIM to guide you. He's waiting.

Now, go be Great!

When You Don't Want To

On the phone with a friend the other day who wasn't happy because a job she'd wanted did not come through. On top of that, a former colleague had requested she come back to her old job just to lead a workshop she was really good at leading.

My friend told me she asked 'What's going on, Lord? I thought that other job was for me? And she said, 'How am I gonna lead a workshop to encourage other people when I need to be encouraged?'

I told her – I feel ya, girl! I don't always want to do an 'inspirational moment'. I'm thinking I NEED to be inspired! But I'm convicted to do it anyway. Then, I told her, someone will message me to say how they needed that inspiration. That let's me know, I'm NOT doing this for me. I'm helping others which ultimately GLORIFIES GOD. In talking to my friend, I was ministering to myself – and I was reminded 1) trust God to guide you even in the disappointment and 2) be obedient brings me closer to God. And God's got a blessing for me.

Now, go be Great!

When Getting The Gift Isn't Enough

Since the pandemic, I'll be honest and admit I've gained a few pounds (I want them off). I was at one of my healthiest times about a year ago when I was working out 4 times a week, eating healthy, etc. I was into it, so I know what it takes to get me back on track again.

And it's not an occasional workout or eating right. I know I have to commit to the lifestyle change. It HAS to be a part of my EVERYDAY. Like God is. But, my devotion today said, I can't just seek God's blessing or what I want to get from Him, and not seek GOD himself.

And God says it so many times in the bible like in

Proverbs 8:17 "I love those who love me and those who seek me find me."

Or Hebrews 11:6 "…He rewards those who earnestly seek him."

So just like I can't lose weight in my spare time, I can't really get to know God (be a faithful follower of God) by giving God my leftovers. I'm reminded I'll give God my first and my best. He will keep his promise. When I SEEK God, I get everything else.

Now, go be Great!

Beyond The Barrel

Over the weekend, I was driving where there was quite a bit of construction. On this particular route, the lane I was in to keep straight shifts after the stoplight. The way it shifts doesn't look like I can keep straight. But normally I can and it's fine.

But this time at the same light where the lane shifts, I could see barrels ahead & it didn't look like I could keep going, so I just sat there for a second thinking 'Oh, my God – can I keep going?!' There are barrels blocking me!! And there was no other car in front of me to help lead the way.

So I took the chance, and kept straight. And sure enough the lane was OPEN beyond the barrel! Whew! I later thought about my hesitancy and not wanting to move ahead because of what I saw. Like in life sometimes I'm not willing to go beyond the barrel. But my devotion today said to keep believing in God no matter what it looks like.

Psalm 30:5 say "weeping may endure for a night, but joy cometh in the morning."

I'm reminded no matter the roadblocks, stay faithful Janine. Like that lane I was in, God can shift things and will move in my favor. I just need to believe.

Now, go be Great!

The God Set-Up

Last week, I posted a series of photos highlighting my 30 years in the radio business. As I looked back at those pictures, I thought about how I even got here. Most people don't know I actually turned down the job to come to Charlotte, for a number of reasons.

Money wasn't right, I didn't know how to run a syndicated show. It was a new concept in black radio so no one really knew and I wasn't a personality perse. I was a reporter who covered hard news. I remembered the program director whom I told no. He literally drove from Charlotte to my job in Raleigh to tell me face to face "You don't understand, this job is for you."

The rest is history. 27 years in Charlotte. The job I said I didn't want. The job I said wasn't me. But, God knew. He's been the road map for me even when I didn't know it. Me being in Charlotte was a God set-up. My devotion today said it -

Psalm 23:3 "He guides me along the right paths…"

I'm reminded keep praying & believing & doing the work. God's got me.

Now, go be Great!

Am I Going The Right Way?

When I went home to Greensboro a few weeks ago, I was riding with my brother to a new restaurant he told me about. It was in an area we weren't familiar with, but my brother insisted he did know of a shortcut. My brother was driving and we got a little turned around. Ok - we got lost.

My brother deviated from the GPS because he was so sure HIS way was the right way. Eventually, we found the spot. Later, I thought about us getting off track. Like I do in life sometimes. Believing & being confident I'm supposed to go one direction, but not checking in with God.

He is the ultimate guide. During my devotion, Isaiah 53:6 says

"All of us like sheep & have strayed away. And leave God's path to follow our own."

BUT, God essentially says in Proverbs 14:12 some paths seem right, but lead to a dead end. I'm reminded, I don't want to be off track & get turned around like my brother and I. I will ask God for help & depend on Him to lead the way

Now, go be Great!

When It's Time To Let Go

I was scrolling through my IG page and saw the video I recorded yesterday of my torn down sandal. I say torn down because it is. The strap that supports my heel and ankle, literally separated from the shoe. A chunk of heel is missing from the sole of the sandal. And another piece is coming unglued from the side of the sandal.

It's a mess, but they are my FAVORITE sandals. I just don't want to let them go, so they've endured all kinds of repairs and my own patch work, including superglue. In my video, I say when it's time to let go.

After watching it again, I realized that was a word for me. How many times in life have I hung on to things I NEED to let go – ol' attitudes, poor habits (like being late or procrastinating, not exercising), dead relationships. In my devotion today, God says in

Isaiah 43:18 & 19 "Forget the former things, don't dwell on the past. I'm doing a NEW THING!"

My worn shoes reminded me, everything has a season. Don't get stuck on the old. Let it go, Janine and LET GOD.

Now, go be Great!

What Channel Are You Listening To?

A friend texted me the other day and asked "What's going on with your station?" Apparently, she heard a lot of static. A short time later, she realized her signal had gotten sketchy as she was headed to the mountains. My friend said she thought she had a wrong station.

I later thought about that — being tuned to the wrong station, wrong channel. Then I thought about NOT being tuned into God. And that can happen sometimes when I'm not sure when He's speaking to me.

My devotion today says God uses different channels to speak to me.

Job 33:14 says "God DOES speak — sometimes one way and another, even though we may not understand it."

My devotion says God speaks though other people, my circumstances, but mostly through the bible. That's where I get the most guidance. I'm reminded, to hear God speak, I must TUNE IN to the right channel — the Bible — EVERYDAY. No sketchy signal like my friend. I'll get on God's frequency.

Now, go be Great!

God Is Still God!

I was at home in Greensboro over the weekend, my mom had gone to church. I stayed home, but felt hungry for some spiritual nourishment. I was feeling kind of blah and needed a strong dose of God.

I remembered my cousin sharing a church Zoom call with me. I was hesitant. You know Zoom calls – poor connection, etc. But, I jumped on. And was so glad I did – it was like it was meant for me.

The sermon was titled "God is STILL God and God is STILL Good!" You know how you think 'Nothing is working out' or 'How am I gonna fix this?' etc. The minister emphasized

Isaiah 55:11, God says "…the words that come out of my mouth, don't come back empty-handed. They WILL do the work I sent them to do. They WILL complete the assignment I gave them."

I thought I don't have to get immersed into what's NOT working. Just because I feel BLAH, doesn't mean God isn't working. He can fix it. I'm reminded just like the sermon I heard that no matter what I'm going through "God is STILL God & God is STILL Good."

Now, go be Great!

What Am I Doing?

Do you ever ask "What am I doing?" Sometimes I feel like I'm all over the place. Doing this and that. I've been praying to God " I just want to be significant. Purposeful." I've even questioned Him "Do you even hear me?"

Fast forward to lunch last weekend. A girlfriend and I were seated outside on a patio when a woman we didn't know approached our table. She squatted down at the table and said, "I don't normally do this…" My friend and I were like "Oh, Lord…" She asked if I were Janine Davis. I said 'Yes' with hesitation.

Then she explained how she'd moved away, battled cancer, was miserable and prayed for God to bring her back to Charlotte so she could 'hear my voice.' I'm thinking "What??" And now she's back in Charlotte, cancer free and felt compelled to tell me "You are walking in your purpose. You are doing what God wants you to do. We love you." I was stunned, my girlfriend was crying. I immediately thanked God for reminding me: You ARE listening, You WILL SHOW UP when I least expect it. And to NEVER give up.

Now, go be Great!

When The Touchdown Is Just Feet Away

I know some of you will find this surprising, but I was actually watching a football game this past Sunday. I was at my brother's that's why. Anyway, there was this one player who was literally just feet away from making a touchdown.

Anyway, as they were setting up the play I'm thinking how in the world is he going get to the goal line because all the other players from the opposing team were so ready to stop him. Well, he clutched the ball to his chest and with his body drilled a hole right down the middle of those players who were trying to stop him. He made a touchdown. I thought unbelievable! He had such determination that NO ONE was going stop him even though they tried.

I thought it's the same kind of determination God wants me to have when fighting the enemy (of negative thoughts, people, situations that seem bleek). My devotion today

Proverbs 3:5-6…God reminded me "Trust in the Lord with all you heart and lean not on your own understanding, In all your ways to submit to Him."

Now, go be Great!

I Almost Fell Into The Trap

I almost fell into the trap. I saw the news story yesterday where the federal government said because of COVID and the recession, it won't be able to pay full benefits of social security – in 2034. I'll have to admit, there was a slight rush of panic that went over me because I heard – NO SOCIAL SECURITY BY 2034!!

I won't even be 70! What am I supposed to do? What should I be doing now? All of this is racing through my head – SEE? The trap. But, then I had my devotion today – Matthew 6:34 when Jesus said (in essence) 'You can't worry about tomorrow today. It's useless.' He said don't worry about tomorrow because it has it's own trouble. And that God helps us WHEN WE TRUST IN HIM – period.'

I'm reminded – Janine no need to fret and worry about something 13 years from now or how you'll make it. God is my ONLY source that is COMPLETELY reliable. I will TOTALLY TRUST IN HIM.

Now, go be Great!

Go Be Great!

A friend told me she was listening to one of my 'Inspirational Moments' and then asked where did I get the phrase "Go Be Great" at the end of each inspiration. I told her my trainer (shout out Roy with Remfit) used to say that to me after each workout.

I told her it stuck with me because of the way it made me feel. I would feel so empowered. I would think he must think I'm great, so therefore I need to go and be that GREAT!

The words took meaning to me personally. GO BE GREAT said to me God has placed GREATNESS in you, Janine. You're not meant to be average. You're God's creation. Now go shine and let others see your shine. Let others see the GOD IN YOU.

Now, go be Great!

My Plants Need Watering Everyday

I've added something to my morning ritual. In addition to my devotion, I now realize I HAVE to water my plants everyday. I love having live plants.

And I have since learned the key to their beauty is regular care. I water them every morning before it gets too hot. I thought I could skip it ONE morning and when I returned home, my plant was so withered looking. It really looked near death. So lesson learned – I HAVE TO WATER MY PLANTS DAILY.

I thought about that. The same way my plants need water every day to survive, so do I NEED GOD EVERYDAY—to survive. I'm thinking 'You know what happens when you DON'T include God EVERYDAY, you get off kilter, disconnected, out of sorts. So, I'm reminded – yes, my plants NEED DAILY nourishment, and I NEED DAILY SPIRITUAL nourishment. I cannot skip God. I NEED HIM EVERYDAY.

Now, go be Great!

I Was Blessed Even Through My Irritation

I received what I thought was a random text this past Sunday. In fact, it was two text messages thanking me for such a powerful word. I was thinking 'Huh?' 'What word?'

Then it hit me. I remembered my co-worker asked me for a favor – literally minutes before I was to start my on-air shift. He and I had just talked about how I need my quiet time in the studio to begin my shift. And there he was STILL in the studio on his cell, TV on and music loud, so I was a bit irritated.

But, I agreed to assist him – though begrudgingly. He didn't specify what I was to do until my mic was on. He'd asked me to pray. I'm thinking I'm fuming, how am I gonna pray? But, I did. And the words that came out were real. As I prayed I actually calmed down. God was reminding me sometimes when I don't want to do the right thing, be obedient. Because in the end, there's a blessing in it. God flipped my agitation into a blessing for me & used it to bless for others through me.

Now, go be Great!

I Can't!

My family and I (meaning me, my brother and cousin) have gotten some extra help for my mom. Yes, she's still active, but we thought having a home health care aide with her a few days a week could be helpful – to get in fitness and as a companion.

It's hard watching a loved one change – moving slower, getting a little more confused. I find myself trying to figure out how to save her -- from aging. From family conference calls to lots of reading on aging to praying, I've done a lot. But after reading my devotion today I realized, I DON'T HAVE TO DO A LOT.

In 2nd Chronicles 20:12, the men of Judah with their families admitted they were helpless facing this large army that was attacking them. They didn't know what to do -- like me trying to save my mom from aging. They felt powerless. But they DID LOOK TO GOD FOR HELP. Because HE IS ALL-POWERFUL, HE IS ALL-KNOWING, so I don't have to be. I'm reminded when I admit to God that I CAN'T, God DOES.

Now, go be Great!

Where's My Sign?

Can I be honest? This being a grown up thing can be exhausting. My mama didn't tell me about all this. The not knowing, the decision making, fear of making wrong decision. Sometimes it can be a bit much.

All those thoughts have been circling in my head as I contemplate next moves. I've been waiting on God to show me something – a sign on which way to go. In my devotion today, it was clear. Stop looking for a sign and start looking at scripture.

And there it was 2nd Chronicles 20:15-18 when King Jehoshaphat was facing THREE armies and knew he couldn't fight against them. He didn't have the power, so he prayed and God said to him "Don't be afraid (Janine) or discouraged by his mighty army. (all your issues). The battle is NOT yours, but God's. YOU won't even need to fight." (chill - what are you fighting for Janine? God's got this). Just then, I found the answer I needed. I'm reminded the sign I was looking for is always there – IN THE WORD.

Now, go be Great!

What's Next?

On the phone with a girlfriend the other day who was really disappointed an opportunity she knew was hers – didn't happen. She got the phrase "we're going in a different direction right now."

She was heartbroken & not sure what to do next. I told her it doesn't mean it's over & to chill. And that I had been reading 2nd Chronicles 20 all week. That's when King Jehoshaphat was met with three armies and he felt powerless and prayed. And God responded, saying don't be afraid, the battle's not yours, no need to fight.

Well, verse 12 says "all the men of Judah and their families were just STANDING at the temple."

STANDING not doing anything because what they faced was too big for them. My devotion said by JUST STANDING they were saying to God 'we don't know what to do next', so we're waiting on you. We are TRUSTING in you, God. I reminded my friend that sometimes DOING NOTHING is faith. So stand still, wait and trust God.

Now, go be Great!

I Need To Give Up

I've been wondering why I have been so exhausted lately. I literally wake up TIRED. I'm thinking – Oh, it's because I haven't been working out, I need to get to bed earlier, drink more water. But after reading my devotion today, I realized it's deeper than that. IT IS ME! I'm not staying in my lane!!

2nd Chronicles 15 says "The battle is not yours, but Gods."

Like I just talked about this scripture last week. Apparently I needed it again. It didn't sink in – until NOW when I RE-READ it. I'm so tired because I've been trying to do GOD'S JOB. (manage my career, my mom's health)

The example in my devotion – it's like me trying to help fly a plane just by flapping my arms while on the plane. That sounds RIDICULOUS. But that's exactly how I've been doing – trying to do things only God is equipped to do. And that's why I'm tired all the time, frustrated and worn out. I'm reminded – Janine, stop trying to FIGHT battles that don't even belong to you. Give it up. They are God's.

Now, go be Great!

When You're Out Of Line

On the phone last night with an ol' radio friend I hadn't talked to in almost a year. We were talking radio and giving each other advice. I kept telling him he has a gift he needs to use.

He agreed and we both pitched each other ideas. We both got excited. I asked him why do you think we're both so excited now. He said because we are doing what God wants us to do. And I asked – how do you know.

He said: because you have joy, there's no stress and the more you do that thing the more it opens up for you. Things start happening, making a way for you to do that thing. I thought about our conversation later and thought maybe I've been stressing because I'm NOT in alignment with what God wants me to do. My devotion:

James 4:7 says "Let God work his will in you."

I'm reminded - to remove the stress, get back in alignment with God.

Now, go be Great!

It's A Trap!

Have you ever been driving and just ready to get to your destination and it seems like EVERYTHING on the road is hindering you? That was me the other day when this dump truck going slow was in front of me on this single lane road.

I wanted to pass it, but I couldn't see what was up ahead, so I didn't want to risk it & wreck.

When I read my devotion today, I realized God CAN SEE AHEAD. He CAN see what I can't see; He CAN see potential danger or traps that lie ahead of me. And when I give Him my attention, He will go ahead of me and show me how to avoid the traps in life.

Psalm 105:4 says "Seek the Lord and his strength, seek his presence continually."

I'm reminded when I can't see what's coming, seek God – all day, every day and in every way.

Now, go be Great!

Getting Rid Of The Gunk

I'm detoxing. And if you've ever detoxed, you know it's not the most pleasant experience. Yea, you always see the results of people who have successfully detoxed, but you never really hear about the "uncomfortable part" it took for them to look and feel great!

When you think about 'detoxing' – it's clearing OUT the gunk and toxins in your body. Years of stuff – unhealthy eating, stress, worry even. It takes time for all that to come out and it's "painful" and "smelly" – if you know what I mean.

I'm in day five, 10 more to go. And as I read my devotion today, I realized my detoxing is a lot like my prayer life. In that before I get my prayers answered, God's going to test me.

Zechariah 13:9 says it. "I will refine them like silver & purify them like gold."

I'm reminded, while it's stressful ridding by body of gunk. Like in life, it's a test. God is purifying me, then blesses me.

Now, go be Great!

When A Squirrel Takes Over

For those of you who follow me on Instagram @jddiva, you have probably seen the videos I've posted showing this pesky squirrel that has tried to take over my balcony. Even though I've just started to share, he's been a 'bother' for past few months.

And I've tried everything to get rid of him. Even recently solicited some of your advice.

But then, I thought, let me just call the 'wildlife' people. I did. They said they'd set a trap, catch him and REMOVE him 5-10 miles away. And they could do that because they have a permit that is required to remove squirrels. Who knew?

Well, THEY DID – because that's what THEY do. They are experts at it. I thought that's the same attitude I should have of God before I try to SOLVE my issues.

Psalm 37:4 says 'He wants to give me the desires of my heart.' But I've got to ask Him.

I'm reminded, just like the wildlife experts know squirrels, God knows ME. I'll pray, honor Him & keep Him FIRST.

Now, go be Great!

Just Getting By

The other night I was so frustrated that my laptop was moving so slow I couldn't get any work done. I'll admit. I have had that warning on my computer for some months saying my disk was full, but ignored it. I was thinking " This is a MAC. I'll delete a few files. It'll be fine."

Well – THIS time is wasn't fine. I couldn't open any site without a substantial delay. One program that I REALLY need to record my commercials, wouldn't record. Finally, I had to stop & research.

Then I found my answer. My cache was clogged with thousands of old files that needed to be deleted. I cleared most of them and my laptop almost ran like new. I thought about how I ignored my computer issue until it no longer worked at it's optimum. Like in life sometimes I have ignored God's word, not been obedient, thinking I can still get by – until I can't. I'm reminded, just like my computer, I cannot operate at my best 'just getting by.' At some point, I have to do what's right & surrender to God & His way. He has all the help I need.

Now, go be Great!

What's The Hold Up?

I like to believe I live in a place of "yes". Meaning, in prayer I have an attitude of anything is possible, ask for what I want and believing I'll receive it. But, right now if I'm being honest, my attitude "What's going on, God?'

Nothing's moving, nothing's shaking right now. I'm struggling to hang on to that attitude of hope and belief – until l I had my devotion this morning.

1st Peter 6-7 says God's strong hand is on you and he'll promote you at the right time.

I've been impatient & misunderstanding God. In my devotion, Pastor Rick Warren says what I see as no movement, God sees I need to slow down. That I'm not ready for what He has coming. I'm reminded of

Habakkuk 2:3 "These things WILL come to pass. Just be patient. They will not be overdue a single day!"

Now, go be Great!

Where'd That Weed Come From?

So I've been so proud of my plants on my balcony. They are growing and staying vibrant except for one. I've noticed a tall strange-looking plant growing right alongside of it.

It's clear it didn't belong there. It was a weed taking over the planter. I'm thinking 'How'd that happen so fast?!' When I read my devotion today, I realized that 'weed' is kind of what I do when I worry. Before I know it, it's taken over me.

In Luke 8:7, Jesus talks about that very thing. He says "the seed that fell among thorns stands for those who hear, but as they go on their way they get choked by life's worries, riches and pleasures."

So when I worry, I'm preoccupied with my problems and pressures of life. They smother me and I don't hear God. I'm reminded, just like my planter, I have to clear out of the weeds in my spiritual life, make room & take time for God, so I can HEAR HIM..

Now, go be Great!

CHAPTER TWO

My To Do List Is Growing

Last night I updated my TO DO list. And I reviewed the things I had crossed off – DONE! I don't know if you're like me, but it's always a good feeling when I can check something OFF MY LIST. But, my 'updated list' grew. Ugh!

And so did my angst. The peace I had in knowing I'd checked things off was quickly interrupted by my thinking 'Will the list ever end?' But during my devotion, I understood it's not the list that's the issue, it's my attitude about conquering the list.

Psalm 34:2 reminded me when things aren't going well, there is God. That "I (should) live and breathe God".

Verse 8 says if I just "open my mouth and taste, open my eyes and see, how good God is & I'm blessed when I run to Him."

I'm reminded there'll always be a THING to get done, but the secret to joy and peace is simple. Know there's a God & Trust Him.

Now, go be Great!

When Things Are Messed Up

I was online reading the news this morning – and got overwhelmed by all the violence, sickness and strife our country is facing right now. Not to mention, my own general life issues. It made me question "Why is everything so MESSED UP?" So I was extra eager to get to my devotion today for relief! And I got it – in

Colossians 1:17 "He is before ALL THINGS and in Him ALL THINGS HOLD TOGETHER."

Meaning when life feels out of control, it isn't. GOD IS IN CONTROL. Even in the midst of pain, sadness and questions.

God is ALWAYS faithful. And when it feels like God is silent & I feel alone in all this, I'm not.

Matthew 28:20 says it. "And surely I am with you always to the very end of age."

I'm reminded, even in the midst of these crazy times when things seem so "messed up", know that there is God. And He IS God OVER the "messed up." And I will TRUST HIM in the midst of it all.

Now, go be Great!

When The Detox Gets Tough

I'm almost finished with this 15-day detox. A few days left. I DO see a difference and I FEEL different, too…but boy was it rough. I can't tell you how many times I said, "That's okay. I'm good. I really don't need to do this. Or question, "Why am I doing this again?"

After one of my 'doubtful' moments, I thought 'Janine, this is a lot like in life.' When things get tough or challenging, you wanna pull back. Give up. I try to avoid the pain and discomfort.

But in my devotion today, I was reminded to look at that THOSE moments of pain or discomfort, as trials of training.

James 1:12 says "God blesses those who patiently endure testing and temptation.

And that in THOSE times, He wants me to lean more on Him.

2nd Corinithians 12:9 says "My grace is all you need. My power works best in weakness."

I'm reminded in difficult times, God is preparing me for greater. That even when it seems like God is breaking me, he's BUILDING ME.

Now, go be Great!

Not Enough Time

I had to have a 'talk' with a friend recently. There was a time we talked practically everyday. But, as life happens the frequency of our conversations changed. Neither one of us could make it happen EVERYDAY. So our everyday talks have now changed to a check in -- twice a month.

I get it. EXCEPT she always has a "request" from me when we do check in. As a friend I don't mind, but it got me thinking is this a real relationship? A real relationship means we communicate regularly & it's not just when one person wants something.

Then I thought – Uh, oh Janine. YOU'VE done that with God. Sometimes YOU just do CHECK IN with Him – it's not EVERYDAY & it's when YOU want something. In that moment, I was reminded before I question my relationship with friends, to check MY relationship with God. Like I want more time with my friends, God wants more of MY time. And HE IS WAITING ON ME.

Now, go be Great!

It's Okay To Be Quiet

Do you ever crave being alone? That was me yesterday. And yes it was my birthday, and yes I got the question several times "What are you doing for you birthday?!!" My response was always the same – "I really don't have an agenda."

All along, I was thinking and FEELING – I really just want to be alone. I think it was my spirit craving aloneness. I believe it was God tugging at me to be alone with Him. Then my devotion confirmed it.

Matthew 6:6 says "Find a quiet, secluded place…be there as simply and honestly as you can. The focus will shift from you to God & you'll begin to sense His grace."

And I did. I had quiet. I had peace and I had God. And I realized in that moment I didn't need excitement to celebrate my birthday. Having time with God was gift more than enough.

Now, go be Great!

When You Don't Know What To Pray For

You ever have so much going on and in your head, you don't even know what to pray for? That was me last night.

And to be honest, I started perusing Instagram. Not looking for anything in particular. Then a video popped up of Angela Rye. You may know her as the savvy sister who is a political commentator on CNN and used to date rapper Common.

Anyway, her message was so on point, I could have sworn she was literally talking to ME. She shared she gave a friend advice that things may be tough right now, but God is always working it out for her HIGHEST good. I let that sink in. Then my devotion TODAY

-- ROMANS 8:28 – that says "all things work together for good to them that love God."

I was reminded, even when things aren't right & I don't even know what to pray for, God is still working it out every detail for my good like that video that popped up. And I say thank you, God – I hear you!

Now, go be Great!

Pop Up Problems

A friend and I went to a pop-up shop recently. It's so cool because what was once an empty space suddenly became this fabulous boutique. The next day in that same space, it was if it were never there .

I thought about that concept of a pop up shop and thought wouldn't it be cool if I handled my worry and stress like that. Meaning when I have an issue – a "pop up problem', but instead of worrying, the FIRST THING I do is PRAY, then it my worry goes away as if IT were never there – like that pop up shop. My worry's there one minute, but by the power of God, it goes away.

And after reading my devotion today, that's what God says about 'worry' anyway. That we're not even supposed to do it because it says we don't trust Him.

Philippians 4:4 & 6 "Don't worry about anything, instead, pray."

I'm reminded as amazing as that pop up shop was, God gives me that instant power – when problems pops up – don't worry, just PRAY.

Now, go be Great!

Back Against The Wall

My recent trip to Turks & Caicos was great, but getting there – STRESSFUL. With all the new travel restrictions we had to get permission to enter the country. I had to submit online paper work from a medical professional that showed I was negative for COVID among other things.

I had to have this before I could even board the plane. It was 1:30 in the morning and no approval. Our flight left at 8am. The panic began. I had not been to sleep at all.

Finally – I just threw up my hands and said I CANNOT CONTROL this! I CANNOT. God's going to work it out.

And he did. By 2:30am I had the authorization I needed to get to Turks & Caicos. I thought later, you did all the stressing and panicking for what, Janine? When your back is against the wall? So what!

Philippians 4:6 & 7… "Don't fret or worry. Instead of worrying, pray."

I'm reminded to remember 'Worry Less, Pray More.' God's got it – every time! Now, BELIEVE.

Now, go be Great!

When I Have To Tiptoe

I have a good friend who sometimes if I'm being honest, I have to tiptoe around him. He's the friend you have to figure out how you plan to ask him a question or how to bring up a topic BEFORE you actually talk to him. Bottom line: He can be a little moody.

Thankfully, when I asked him about joining an upcoming Zoom call he replied, "Yes!" WHEW! I thought he's cool, but I hate that I never know what I'm going to get with him. During my devotion, I thought about that. I thought I'm glad I don't have to worry about that with God. He's NOT sometimey.

James 1:17 says, "Every good and perfect gift is from above, coming down from the Father, who does NOT change like shifting shadows."

God is NOT moody like my friend. God is consistent. And He's faithful. And I'm reminded, I NEVER have to prep to talk to God. He is the ONLY one who will act the same towards me no matter what.

Now, go be Great!

When There's No Pep In Your Talk

A girlfriend and I were on the phone the other night giving each other a pep talk. Each was trying to give the other advice on best course of action, ideas, encouragement, etc. I think the more we talked, the more we got frustrated. Finally, we ended our conversation with no real resolve.

I just went in my closet, tired of thinking, figuring it out. Before I knew it and I was saying OUT LOUD "I CAN'T!" Then I thought, "I shouldn't." God led me to my devotion today—which I've read before.

Proverbs 3:5-6 "Trust GOD from the bottom of your heart, Janine. DON'T try to figure out everything on your own.….Don't assume you know it all – RUN TO GOD!"

I immediately thought – Janine, you're doing it again. Thinking YOU have to figure it out. God is reminding me… all I have to REALLY do is "Go to Him & listen to HIS voice in everything I do. He's going to keep me on track. I will RUN to God!

Now, go be Great!

I Was Afraid To Ride The Wave

While in Turks & Caicos, I road on a catamaran – basically a large boat. When I got on, me and colleague went to the bottom of the boat and some went on the 2nd level. It had the best view of the ocean!

After riding for a few minutes, I wanted to go up top but I was hesitant because standing and riding the waves made it harder to keep your balance. But I didn't want to miss out on THAT VIEW!

I pushed through my doubt and found a spot where I could lean against the boat, steady myself and feel secure. During my devotion, I thought about that & how I almost let doubt & my insecurity steal the joy in seeing the ocean. I thought like I do in riding the waves of life sometimes… allowing fear or doubt to keep me from moving forward. But God has the power to steady me, hold me and lift me up. I'm reminded in

Psalm18:32 , "It is God who arms me with strength and keeps my way secure."

I will believe ALL THINGS are possible through Him.

Now, go be Great!

Am I Really Listening?

I was on the phone with my cousin recently. I'm an active listener. So while she's talking I'm saying my "uh-huh's" "right, rights", etc. At one point, I was talking. My cousin is NOT an active listener, so it's silent as I'm talking. So silent, sometimes I think the call has dropped so in haste, I'll say "Hello? Are you there?"

She'll reply calmly, "Yes, I'm listening." We both laughed about how I go into panic mode when I'm talking, she's silent & I think she's not there. But, I thought about that. I do that with God, too. When it seems like he's not answering me or isn't there? I go into panic mode.

In my devotion today, it says different. That when God is silent it doesn't mean he's NOT present.

Psalm 37:7 says "Surrender yourself to the Lord, and wait patiently for him".

I'm reminded, God's silence is my TEST. Instead of panicking, I'll let go of control & TRUST GOD.

Now, go be Great!

When I'm Tempted!

I was planning for a weekly meeting with a friend who's helping me with a few projects, specifically my 'Yasssss, hunni!' clothing wear. We agreed we'll need more inventory for the fall. I immediately thought – this is so not a good time for this!

Spend MORE MONEY! How is this gonna happen? Do I even need to do it all? Maybe I shouldn't do it!

During my devotion today, I realize my thought of giving up is a temptation the enemy uses to hinder my success. Thoughts like "This is too hard", "I don't have the money to do this" "I'm not qualified" "Who's gonna help me" - I said all those. I was TEMPTED to give up. But God says in

Luke 22:40 "Pray you don't enter into temptation."

I reminded, to even think about giving up is the work of the enemy. My prayer: God, help me recognize the temptation to give up & resist.

Now, go be Great!

Can I Get My Order To Go?

I was reminiscing about my recent visit to Turks & Caicos and realized one of the reasons I liked it so much – besides the water and weather – was the PEOPLE. They were so accommodating. Everything was "yes" and "of course".

They just made me feel like there was nothing I couldn't have. "Can I get my order to go and take it to the beach." Sure, no problem. "Can I order a 2nd entrée." Absolutely, no problem. No request was ridiculous. Nothing seemed impossible.

When I had my devotion today – I thought Janine that is how GOD operates. And wants you to feel about Him.

James 1:17 says "Every good and perfect gift is from above."

And Matthew 7:11 says "If you know how to give good gifts to your children, how much more will your Father give good gifts to those WHO ASK."

I'm reminded God wants to give me everything I need – He has unlimited resources. I just need to ask. (James 4:2 "You don't have because you don't ask God")

Now, go be Great!

Worry Less, Pray More

I was on the phone with my brother the other day just catching up. He asked what did I want the family to do for the holidays. I immediately thought and said 'HOLIDAYS?' I haven't even gotten to this weekend!

We both laughed, but I was serious. I later thought with so much to be concerned about RIGHT NOW – work, my mom, bills – how do I even begin to think about happenings a month or two from now. Then, as I read my devotion today, God thinks the same way.

Philippians 4:6-8 says I'm not supposed to WORRY about anything and instead, PRAY about everything.

And Matthew 6:34 "I shouldn't WORRY about tomorrow (Thanksgiving, Christmas)…because tomorrow has its own worries."

I'm reminded not to get worked up about holiday plans, Janine. God wants me to simply TRUST HIM and TRUST HIM ONE DAY AT A TIME.

Now, go be Great!

Rich To Give

A girlfriend told me the other day that she misses my inspirational moments on video. I hadn't done the video version in a minute. She asked me why? I was honest and told her, it got to be too much… I said I'm not able. I was trying to make it perfect.

She said why does that matter? And then recalled one of the inspirational moments I did ON VIDEO that really touched her. Then I was touched.

When I had my devotion today – that touched me, too. 2nd Corinthians 9:10-12 essentially says God will supply you with all the seed and bread you need to produce a rich harvest to give away (like my videos). He'll always make you rich enough to be generous. So I thought doing my VIDEO inspiration is not about me, it's meeting the needs of people, its helping me grow spiritually AND it's bringing glory to God. I'm reminded, God not only GIVES to me, He wants to give THROUGH me.

Now, go be Great!

What Is My Daily Bread?

A friend and I were talking about fasting and what it does for the your body. I know "fasting" is abstaining from food or drink but at the root of "fasting" is denying yourself of things that normally bring you comfort or some sort of satisfaction.

After talking with my friend, I realized I did not want to 'fast' right now. I didn't want to feel hungry. But after reading my devotion today, I realized it's not just FOOD I need to keep me full.

Deuteronomy 8:3…says "People don't live by bread alone. They LIVE by every word that comes from the mouth of the Lord."

My devotion referenced when the children of Israel were walking to the Promised Land and had no food. God dropped food from heaven to show them they need more than food to live. They needed to DEPEND ON HIM – like me. So, I'm reminded I DO need physical food to live, but REAL LIVING comes when I get spiritual nourishment, too. And FEED on the word of God.

Now, go be Great!

My Assessment

I just started working out again with a new trainer. And before we started, she had a series of exercises she wanted me to do to see my areas of strengths and weaknesses or where I needed to improve. She had to 'assess' where I was. Reading my devotion today, it focused on 'seeing where I am' with God – having a spiritual assessment. I had to ask myself "Are there some areas in your life Janine, where you know you're wrong & those habits & hang ups keep me living God's BEST life for me?"

Psalm 139: 23 & 24 says to ask God to "Search me….point out anything in me that offends God and lead me to a path of everlasting life."

My devotion even noted I should write down those things that may be holding me back; things not pleasing to God. I'm reminded, just as serious as I am in assessing my physical health to FEEL my best, I pray to God to assess my spiritual health – so I can LIVE God's best for me.

Now, go be Great!

Am I In The Wrong Line?

When I was in the airport last month I was approaching the airlines check-in. I had to check my bags. Of course the lines were long, so naturally I just walked to the PRIORITY area that had NO line. As soon as I approached, the airline staff person asked "Are you FIRST CLASS?" I wasn't, but said, "Yes – I'm PRIORITY."

He then proceeded to check me in as well as my bags. As I had my devotion today, I thought about my level of confidence walking to the PRIORITY line. My ticket wasn't, but in my head I WAS and AM PRIORITY. And God thinks so, too!

He BELIEVES that about me. And wants me to BELIEVE in him. Make Him a priority. BELIEVE because as Titus 1:2 says "He's a God who CANNOT LIE." BELIEVE because in

Psalm 80:3" he can restore me…"

– my finances, relationships, faith, health. I'm reminded that same confidence I had walking to the airline PRIORITY line is the same confidence and BELIEF I should have in God's power over my life. I will make him a PRIORITY.

Now, go be Great!

When You Need To Power Down

I was on my laptop late last night and it was processing slowly again. I've already deleted tons of files and even moved some to my hard drive. But this time, I decided Janine why don't you just cut if off. The one thing I hadn't done - power down the computer.

Today – when I turned it back on, it was almost like NEW. It processed quickly, no buffering. I'm thinking 'that's all it needed? Just to power down?'

When I read my devotion today, I realized there are times when I NEED to POWER DOWN. When life gets overwhelming, and I feel burdened with decision-making, & responsibilities – there is God. And He says it in

Matthew 11:28 "Come to Him, if you're weary and burdened and He'll give me rest."

I'm reminded there is POWER in POWERING DOWN and being still before God. He can restore me and make ME like NEW.

Now, go be Great!

That Aggie Pride!

This weekend is Homecoming for my Alma Mater – NC A&T "Aggie Pride". I can remember in my early college years, our football team wasn't so great! In fact, we kinda sucked. But, the crazy thing was – it didn't matter. You'd never know we had a losing team because we were always so hyped.

We celebrated with the same vim, vigor and passion when we lost as when we'd won. The singing, shouting and stepping went on WIN or LOSE.

I thought about the AGGIE PRIDE and thought 'It's that attitude I should have when I face problems & troubles' – instead of getting sad or mad, I should immediately fix my eyes on God and His goodness and PRAISE HIM. My devotion today

Psalm 34:1 & 2 says "I will bless the LORD at all times; I live & breathe God."

I'm reminded the same AGGIE PRIDE I have win or lose, is the same attitude I'll adopt when afflictions come my way. I won't be defeated; I won't give up, instead I'll PRAISE GOD!

Now, go be Great!

My List Is Out Of Whack

I devote a few days of the week to work on my personal goals. I was reviewing my list. And by the 10th 'GOAL', I sat back & thought "How will I ever get all this done?"

I recalled a similar exercise I did once with my executive coach where I shared my list of goals. One of them included having a stronger relationship with God. My coach pointed out he thought it was interesting I had my God goal last on my list.

Then he asked me rather casually "What do you think would happen if I put God as the first goal?" He suggested "Seems like all the other goals would fall into place." I paused at the time and thought, "Wow". In my devotion today, Jesus was just as blunt in telling the disciples how to have eternal life.

Mark 10:27 "No chance at all if you think YOU can pull it off by yourself. EVERY CHANCE if you LET GOD do it."

So, I'm reminded to GET ALL MY GOALS DONE, re-prioritize my list. And to put God back FIRST.

Now, go be Great!

Getting What I Want

My cousin and I went out to eat and it had taken quite a long time to get our order. The server came by to apologize for the delay and to say our order would be out shortly.

Before she left, I suggested to the server "How about an appetizer on the house while we wait?"

She obliged us – and actually brought us TWO appetizers – on the house, of course. My cousin chuckled and said "How'd you do that?" I told her, "Ask for what you want." I thought about that later – that I try to practice that with God, too. In fact,

Matthew 7:7 says it. "Don't bargain with God. Be direct. Ask for what you need."

I'm reminded I am a child of God, Janine and He wants to give to me. No negotiation necessary.

Now, go be Great!

I Couldn't Fight It

Some friends and I took their 4-year-old niece trick-or-treating. And did I mention I'm trying to get back on my healthy regimen? Well, let's just say the healthy regimen went out the door. Sooooo much candy – and of course I was tempted to divulge.

I tried to resist, but I wasn't very successful. When I read my devotion today, I was fighting temptation the wrong way. Pastor Rick Warren says 'You don't FIGHT temptation. You just REFOCUS.' Because whatever gets my attention, gets me. I think about it, my feelings kick in & then I act on it.

Psalm 119:6 says, "Thinking about your commands will keep me from doing some foolish thing."

So, I'm reminded whatever my temptation (food, not exercising, people & relationships), the key is NOT to push back, but to change the way I think. Put my mind on something else. Put my mind on Christ.

Now, go be Great!

Expect The Shift

I was watching a movie the other night and this man was creating a video to post on YouTube. He was so detailed & very particular in creating it. He completed his video and posted it. Well, later on we learn his video that he spent so much time creating only garnered one view.

Needless to say, he was hurt, sad and just gave up hope. I'm thinking 'Come on bruh, it's just a video.' But another part of me could understand. When you have those moments, like this character, where you don't see how things could possibly turn around. I mean he had one view! My devotion today, turned me around.

Proverbs 29:18 essentially says 'You have to have vision or you'll die. But if I put my TRUST in God, have HOPE in Him, I'll be blessed."

I'm reminded, even when things don't seem as if they will turn around, like that characters one view on YouTube, I should EXPECT the shift; BELIEVE in it. And have hope in something BIGGER than me – My Hope IS GOD.

Now, go be Great!

When You're Tired Of Figuring It Out

I missed my 6:15 morning workout. I overslept. My trainer was okay with it, saying I was probably just really tired. Honestly, I felt guilty. But, I thought about it later and thought I HAVE BEEN exhausted, NOT physically, but mentally.

I had fallen back into my trap of 'trying to figure things out' again. And THAT'S exhausting. When I read my devotion, I could see it. I've been depending on ME way too much.

1st Corinthians 4:20 says "For the Kingdom of God is NOT just a lot of talk, it is LIVING by God's power."

And my devotion said to get God's power in my life by,

1) I GOTTA pray – the two (God's power & prayer) go together.
2) I gotta take risks to obey God – even if they're scary & don't make sense.
3) And I can't give up when things get rocky – God is teaching me to TRUST HIM.
So, I'm reminded, NO guilty feelings because of a missed workout. And NO giving up. Instead, I'll GIVE IN & surrender to God's power. He's waiting to BLESS ME.

Now, go be Great!

I Don't Need The Music

I made my morning workout with my trainer. (shout out Bre) Anyway, we went to an area with few people – on purpose. There were about five or six others in the room. It was quiet and you can feel the focus. I liked it.

As I started my circuit, my trainer put on music from her phone. It played for about 5 minutes, before she switched up the music. She asked did I like that song. I said, "Honestly, I don't have to have music." She said, "Hey, if it's a distraction, I'll get rid of it.". I thought – I NEED to practice that. I get distracted by technology, other people, my own plan.

I thought when these things consume me, I drift away from God. I get distracted like hearing that music during my workout. During my devotion, it said 'Don't let the noise of the world keep you from hearing the voice of the Lord.' I'm reminded to get rid of the noise & put my focus on God.

Now, go be Great!

When I Get Annoyed

My 23 year-old-niece called me last night. When I answered the phone, I could hear her talking to someone else WHILE she's calling me. Millennials. Anyway, I slightly annoyed, said 'Hello' again. She said 'Hold on. I'm trying to get you to hear what this man is saying to me.'

Apparently, it was a bogus sales person trying to get my mom to buy something. My niece was at my moms intercepting the call. I thought 'Good, she's handling it.' Until she started asking me a barrage of questions while the sales guy was still on the phone. So I'm flustered, he's talking, she's trying to explain. Then I just stopped talking.

And I remembered my devotion on wisdom.

Proverbs 2:6 says "God gives us wisdom. From His mouth comes knowledge & understanding."

I thought God wants me to use wisdom right now. Be patient & wait. So that's why I stopped talking, settled down & listened to my niece. She handled the call. I was reminded, to take the emotions out, Janine & use the wisdom God gave you to do what's right.

Now, go be Great!

When I Need To Exhale

So, I was on the phone with my cousin and she was telling me about a new tactic she's added to the graduate class she teaches at UNCC (University of North Carolina — Charlotte). She says students are really stressed when they get to class, so she introduced a breathing exercise at the start of each class to help ease their stress.

She explained you inhale, then slowly exhale letting your body completely relax. As you breathe out, she said you envision all the stress & anxiety leaving your body – your eyes, neck, shoulders, back and so forth. It sounded inviting, so I started to do it.

I could literally feel my tension ease up. It was a relief. Then when I read my devotion, that's the kind of relief I can always get with God. Who tells me in

Psalm 46:10 "Let go of my concerns…"

That means health, mom's health, bills, my future…I'm reminded that every day I have a choice on who will be in control of my life. I will let God be God.

Now, go be Great!

When You Don't Know

A friend asked me how am I feeling about almost going into a new year. I told her I'm optimistic, but I really don't know what next year is going to hold for me. And I really didn't like saying "I don't know", but when I read my devotion said today, NOT knowing isn't a bad thing.

In fact, admitting 'I don't know' is the beginning of faith. I realized it's acknowledging I DON'T know everything and that there are things at work in my life and around me that are beyond my understanding. And that's okay.

> *In Isaiah 55:8-9. God says "My thoughts are nothing like your thoughts; My ways are far beyond anything you could imagine."*

So even God's lowest thoughts are still HIGHER than my best plans. I'm reminded my "I don't know's" or "I'm not sures" don't cancel out faith. It's okay NOT to know as long as I TRUST that God DOES.

Now, go be Great!

I Didn't Make The Stop

I was on the phone as I was driving the other day and planned to make a stop before I got home. The plan was to go to the post office, and the next thing I knew I was parking in my parking garage. No post office.

Have you ever done that? Been driving, not paying full attention and not even remembering how you got where you were? Crazy! Obviously it was a habit to go the home route – it was my normal routine. I didn't even think about the steps, my route, my plan to stop. I just went with it.

And I realized later that's how I should go with the flow of God and follow His steps for me. And that's what He wants me to do.

Proverbs 4:12 says "When you walk, your steps shall not be hampered; when you run, you shall not stumble."

I'm reminded, when I ask God for guidance, BELIEVE He's keeping me safe even when I'm not paying attention. I WILL BELIEVE he keeps me following the right path.

Now, go be Great!

What Am I Waiting For?

I have this thing I do and I've got to STOP! I just did it yesterday after work. I was to go walking, but instead decided I'd do it in the morning. A friend asked me to write her a recommendation. There's no rush on it, but I said I'd do it in a couple of weeks.

That thing I do – is procrastination. And after reading my devotion today, I realized Jesus doesn't like it. In fact, He talks about it specifically in

Luke 9:62 when HE said "No procrastination. No backward looks. You can't put God's kingdom off until tomorrow. Seize the day."

I thought about how that applies to my life. Not just walking or writing a letter. It's living in the NOW and ACTING in the NOW. Getting IT done NOW! Because I know tomorrow isn't promised. I thank God for that nudge because I am reminded to end the procrastination, Janine. DO the "IT" NOW!

Now, go be Great!

Give Up The Fight

Some co-workers and I were laughing at another co-worker who refuses to get with technology. Yes, he's a little older, but he won't even check his email. Do you know how much information you can miss by NOT checking emails?!

We were teasing him because he is relentless in NOT giving up the fight. I told him, "Stop making it hard on yourself. And just give in! Technology isn't going anywhere!"

I thought about what I said later during my devotion. I think that's probably what God says to me. 'Stop making it hard on yourself, Janine. Why are YOU trying to solve all YOUR issues – finances, the job, your future. Why don't YOU just give in?! I'm here and I'm NOT going anywhere.' I'm reminded just like I told my co-worker to stop fighting technology – I need to give up on my own fight and give in to GOD.

Now, go be Great!

I Voided A Check

I recently had to write a VOIDED check to set up a new bank account. I know – when's the last time you actually wrote a check? Anyway, I know once VOID is written on the check, the check has NO MONETARY VALUE.

It's a simple thing – a VOIDED CHECK – but I thought about it during my devotion.

Isaiah 55:11, when God says "the words that come out of my mouth, don't come back empty-handed or void. They do the work I sent them to do. They complete the assignment I gave them."

I thought about that & had to say out loud – Thank you, God – for that reassurance. Just as I was about to doubt, be uncertain about what's next, work, family, whatever…God corrected my thinking. And reminded me His Word never comes back empty. His Word is Power. His word does have VALUE. His Word can CHANGE a thing OR MAKE a thing. His word just IS and I will BELIEVE in it.

Now, go be Great!

Who Am I Waiting For?

As a homeowner, I wanted to take advantage of the low interest rates a few months ago. In fact, I told my cousin my plan to refinance my refi. She got excited and did it! Bam! She refinanced.

Again, that was a couple of months ago. Mine still hasn't happened!! I'm like "What is the hold up???!" My lender assures me it'll happen by the end of the month. You know what I realized? I'm NOT GOOD at the waiting game.

When I read my devotion today, I also realized I'd gotten away from WHO I'm waiting on and the MEANING behind the wait.

Psalm 27:14 says plainly "Wait on the Lord, Janine & be of good courage. He'll strengthen you."

So, I was reminded – you're not WAITING on the mortgage lender, Janine. You're WAITING on God and His perfect timing. AND I'M TRUSTING He WILL MOVE on my behalf when it's time.

Now, go be Great!

Stick With It

I've changed up my workout strategy a bit. Other than the gym and a trainer, I've committed to walking – at least two or two and a half miles, five days a week. And I'm doing it! I'm in week number 2.

Now, I will say with my trainer & the gym, it seems like there was a noticeable difference after the second week. The walking – not so much. A friend, who is an avid walker & who lost 20lbs walking said, "Just stick with it, Janine. You'll see."

My devotion today said something similar.

Pslam119:2. "You're blessed when you stay on course, walking steadily on the road revealed by GOD. You're blessed when you follow His directions, doing your best to find HIM. Don't go off on your own."

I was reminded my commitment to walk isn't just about my 'walking', it's more about my commitment to walk the course of life that God has for me. I'm reminded stay the course, Janine. God has your walk set.

Now, go be Great!

I Don't Want A New Printer

I found out the other day the new wireless router I have isn't compatible to my printer. Translation: my printer is too old to connect to the NEW router.

I did not want to purchase a NEW PRINTER. In fact, I refuse. My printer still works – ok it's 10 years old. I thought: I CAN KEEP it, and I WON'T print. Or I can accept there's a new way for it to connect via my NEW router, so I CAN print.

My devotion today Numbers 14:3 when the Israelites decided they wanted captivity in Egypt rather than freedom in the Promised Land. They questioned God "Why is the Lord taking us to this country to have us die in battle? Wouldn't it be better for us to return to Egypt?" I thought about that in my life – when I choose the old way (like sticking with my old printer) versus the new (God's will).

I'm reminded, to have the courage like Caleb to face the challenges of the NEW with God's help. And not give in to the comfort of the old way (my old printer) I will trust God and follow HIS WAY for my life.

Now, go be Great!

Stop Questioning, Start Trusting

Have you ever been praying to God, but your prayer is full of questions to Him? That was me the other day. God why hasn't my mortgage refinance gone through yet? Why does my mom have to lose her memory? Am I ever gonna get paid what I'm worth?

And I'm thinking to myself – I'm honest, I try to be good to be people. I just sighed and said I don't get it! Then I read my devotion. Job 42: 2-3 and 6. Job had already lost everything – family, health, wealth and questioned God about his losses.

In Chapter 42, Job STOPS asking God why. Job said, "I know you can do anything and no one can stop you." Job admitted he had talked about things over his head. And then told God he takes it all back. I reminded to be like Job when life gets hard & I don't understand, remember who God is – He's loving, all powerful, in control and will protect me. I'll stop questioning God & start trusting Him.

Now, go be Great!

Beyond The Grief

This week I received disturbing news that two people I knew had passed away. One in, particular hit me surprisingly hard. I hadn't seen him in years, though I'd communicated with him via text. And I was giving him props on his latest work.

I learned he'd had a stroke. And like many of us had his share of up's and down's and had been really stressed. I immediately went into guilt mode. WHY didn't I know, WHY didn't I check on him, WHY didn't I CALL instead of text?

I was looking back at some past devotions and notes I'd taken and saw this: "Grief is an opportunity to put your faith into action." And I thought about MY FAITH and how it shouldn't surface just when life is going great! But, it's for times like now, when there's doubt and pain, Janine. Remember

Proverbs 3:5 "Trust God. Don't try to figure out everything on your own. Listen for God's voice."

I will seek Him.

Now, go be Great!

Give Up The Fight

(THE SQUIRREL CHRONICLES)

I continue to battle with the infamous squirrel that is in love with my balcony. I have to be honest, I HAVE been praying for God to let me know why this squirrel is relentless in coming on my balcony.

I've tried all kinds of methods to deter him. I removed the pillow & plants, sprinkled cayenne pepper. I've chased him off and finally used Cajun black pepper. I thought that did it. It didn't. Yesterday, he came back and SAT on my outdoor sofa and looked at me as I sat inside watching TV. I just sighed and said 'I give up.' When I had my devotion this morning, I thought maybe that's what God wants me to do.

1st Peter 5:6-8 says "Humble yourselves under the mighty hand of God, that he may exalt you in due time. Cast all your cares upon HIM. Be sober and vigilant."

I thought, be VIGILANT Janine, like that squirrel. Is God saying to me keep asking, seeking, knocking Janine? Like the squirrel, don't allow obstacles to get in my way? Maybe that squirrel is a message for me to stop all the fretting over it, like I do in life Janine. God is reminding me to give up the fight & submit to Him. Relax in God & Trust Him.

Now, go be Great!

The Power Of Powering Down

I've been trying to get my Google Home device connected so I can play music in my bedroom. It wouldn't connect to my Wi-Fi. Then I remembered I'd gotten a new router. And my Google Home wasn't connected to it.

I had connected it before & figured this will be easy. Not so much! After a few failed attempts, I finally sought instruction. The first instruction, unplug the Google Home device. Power it down. I did. Then it worked.

When I read my devotion today –

Matthew 11:28-30 when Jesus said "Come to me all you are weary and burdened, I will give you rest…For my yoke is easy and burden light."

In my quest to get my device working again, all it needed was to power down. Like I need to do when burdens & worry seep in. I'm reminded of the power of quiet, listening, expecting and receiving from God. I will exchange my worry for His peace.

Now, go be Great!

So What If I'm Getting Older

I met with my financial planner the other day mapping out my retirement plan. It's crazy to think in 15 years I'll be 70! People are living longer now. The CDC says the life expectancy in the U.S. is 78 years old.

After our meeting, I thought if I believe the CDC, I'll have another 23 years to live. I know God has the final say, but I did think I'll be 78!! And what can I really get done at that age?

After reading my devotion,

Joshua 14:10.says The Israelites had refused to settle in the Promised Land because they said it was too hard so they ended up wandering in the desert for 40 years. Joshua & Caleb believed God's promise.

After 40 years, Caleb said he was 85 years old, still strong and ready to fight. He wanted the country God promised. He was still on a mission for God. And Moses was 80 when God told him to set His people free. I'm reminded, I may stop working, but I can keep serving God. And it's never too late to answer His call on my life.

Now, go be Great!

Built For This

I was watching a Netflix movie last night called "Bruised". It starred Halle Berry who plays a washed up fighter who lost her desire to fight and her coach kept pushing her to get back in the ring.

A phrase he said stuck with me. He said "You are MADE for this. You are BUILT for this." That stuck with me because I can remember the time I felt like Halle's character and I was "done with radio." In fact, I walked away from radio for about 4 years.

Reading my devotion –

Ephesians 2:10 says "For we are God's handiwork, created in Jesus to do good works, which God prepared in advance for us to do."

I realized that when God puts something in me – an ability, a gift -- it's in me. I can't escape it. I can try as Halle did in the movie and I did in real life…but God has MADE me for THIS – what I'm doing. I'm reminded He did it, so I can glorify Him and STAY in it.

Now, go be Great!

When You're Restless

Have you ever had one of those SOLID SLEEPS? I mean, when you wake up you say "Dang, I slept good!" I said, "Thank you, God!" I feel so rested!!

And I have to say, I've been checking my balcony for the past few days and NO signs of Rocky the squirrel. Like NONE at all. I'd like to believe that what I said earlier is true – that Rocky was a symbol of my worry; me trying to manage EVERYTHING in my life & getting frustrated doing it. That God was signaling me to 'give up the fight'. Not just with Rocky, but with handling my LIFE.

I'd like to believe that as soon as I decided to stop worrying about Rocky, stop the fight -- he went away. My devotion today said trusting God allows me to enter his REST & be confident HE's fighting my battles. I'm reminded HE WILL solve my problems, HE WILL meet my needs. I WILL continue to TRUST GOD – COMPLETELY.

Now, go be Great!

When It's Dark & The Road Is Winding

I had a great girlfriend quick getaway this weekend. A girlfriend and I went to an island. My girlfriend drove and at night it was pretty dark. The road was winding and animals were lurking on the road, too – like possums and raccoons.

I was in charge of giving her directions from the GPS. My girlfriend was cheerfully driving & singing along to music that was pumping. I'm thinking we are going pretty fast to NOT know where we were going. I needed the music lower and driving slower. I asked my girlfriend, 'How can you focus?'

She laughed and said , "I'm not worried. I'm confident you're gonna give me directions. I know you'll tell me to turn when I need to turn." I thought about that later & thought, "Ha! That's exactly how God wants us to have confidence in Him. He wants us to allow Him to guide us without worry – just like my girlfriend. I'm reminded even when the road seems dark and uncertain, I can still be confident God will guide me.

Now, go be Great!

When You Can't Escape The Wreckage

On the phone with a girlfriend a few weeks ago who was telling me her daughter had gotten into a car wreck. She wasn't seriously hurt, but her car was totaled.

I just talked to the same girlfriend the other day and she mentioned her same daughter got carjacked. I was stunned. Again, she was not hurt.

My girlfriend questioned what God was doing with her daughter – her car wreck & now car jacking. And both incidents she was unscathed. During my devotion, I thought God is doing what He does.

Corinthians 4:8 & 9 says "We are troubled on every side, yet not distressed…perplexed, but not in despair, cast down, but not destroyed."

I'm reminded even in the wreckage of life, like with my girlfriend's daughter, God is there in the wreckage with us. And He will NEVER leave us.

Now, go be Great!

Why Is This Happening?

I woke up this morning thinking about TV personality and now talk show host Nick Cannon. He recently lost his 5 month old son to brain cancer. He talked about it on his talk show.

It was obviously difficult for him to get it out on national TV, but Nick did. One thing he said stood out to me. He still trusts God. I thought imagine suffering that kind of loss and still trusting God.

I'm certain Nick Cannon is asking why did I have to lose my baby boy? Five months? Brain cancer? What parent ever understands losing a child? But, my devotion today said --trust God even when you don't understand what's happening in your life and have questions. For me it's 'What does my future hold? Will I get married?' I'm reminded, instead of stressing & demanding explanations, I'll give it to God & I will trust Him whether he explains it or not.

Now, go be Great!

My Headache Is Gone

I don't get headaches often, but if I feel one coming on, I'll quickly take a Goody headache powder. They work wonders and so fast. I felt a headache coming on recently and I had my remedy – popped a Goody, headache gone.

I thought about that later during my devotion today. As quickly as I threw that Goody powder down my throat to avoid a headache, I need to go to God when I start to worry, have doubt or fear or anxiety.

Phillipians 4: 6-7 says it. "It's wonderful what happens when Christ displaces worry at the center of your life."

So, I'm reminded just like I have an instant remedy for my headache – I go get Goody's, there's an antidote for my worry and life's obstacles – I go get God.

Now, go be Great!

Where Will I Wear It?

I was in my closet the other night on the phone with my hairstylist and showed him a couple of new outfits I bought. He liked them and said, "Where are you going with those outfits? " I said I don't really know. I just bought them. I said I'm sure I'll have somewhere to go with them.

We both laughed, but he agreed. In fact, it led him to recall a word he heard from Bishop TD Jakes. He said Bishop Jakes says to operate as if you already have whatever is. Like my new outfits – setting the stage for the blessing that is to come.

I thought about that for my everyday life – that my attitude should be one of expectancy. My devotion today –

Psalm 27:14 says it "Wait for and confidently EXPECT the Lord. Take heart. Don't' Quit. Stay with God."

I'm reminded, having an attitude of expectancy is to live anticipating the blessings of God.

Now, go be Great!

Completing The Transaction

I've been doing my online Christmas shopping and in one store, I put an item in a shopping cart, but didn't purchase yet. It's on a virtual hold. Well, of course you know that store WILL REMIND you that item you chose, but didn't buy is STILL THERE.

In fact, I received an email today from the store where my item is still on virtual hold stating that, "We saved your order for you." And the messages continue. Another one said "We noticed you still have an item in your cart. No rush, thought you'd like to know." And another message: "Go ahead, treat yourself!"

I thought this store is determined for me to complete my transaction, to stop holding out and remove the item from virtual hold to purchased. During my devotion, I thought do I sometimes hold out on GOD? NOT fully commit to Him, like I'm doing with my shopping cart item.

Matthew 6:33 says to "seek first the kingdom of God and His righteousness & all these things will be added to you."

I'm reminded God never puts His love for me on hold; it's always there, He's ready to bless me. I just need to continue to 'complete the transaction' wit Him.

Now, go be Great!

It's So Dark Out Here

My girlfriends and I spent the weekend at the home of another girlfriend – as a quick girls getaway to rejuvenate. Anyway, she lives a ways out and all of us talked about how dark it was while traveling to her house.

Not a street light in sight. It was pitch dark. Not to mention it was raining that night and difficult to see. And I'm a pretty good driver, but even I was a little shaky. But, we made it – safe & sound.

Meanwhile, the next morning at my girlfriends house, the sun was shining so bright. She has tons of windows. I thought it's amazing just how hours before, we were anxious because it was so dark we could barely see in front of us. During my devotion today

John 8:12 Jesus says "I am the world's Light. No one who follows me stumbles around in the darkness. I provide plenty of light to live in."

I was reminded… in life, in my moments of darkness (anxiety, doubt), I can have no fear because when I go to God & He will always light my way.

Now, go be Great!

Who Am I Investing In?

As 50+, I'm focused on living out the second half of my life. For example, I'm more conscious about my spending habits and my investing habits, too. My financial planner suggested stocks and mutual funds.

And I recently signed up for a personal development class, too. It's to enhance my skill set. But if I'm being honest, I actually hesitated to sign up for the class. I paused and even asked myself if this too much money? Do I really need it?

In my devotion today, I learned that's what God wants me to do. Invest in myself. He says it this way…

2nd Peter 3:18 "Grow in spiritual strength and become better acquainted with Jesus."

So, I'm reminded no need to feel guilty about investing in me. When I invest in me, I invest in my personal growth. It's investment in my spiritual growth. Like God wants – to become a better me is an investment in my character to become more like Jesus.

Now, go be Great!

I Can Do It!

I attended a meeting the other day to strategize on making improvements to my neighborhood. In the past, we as homeowners have tried a number of strategies (ways to keep it safe, clean & peaceful).

We've talked to city representatives, real movers & shakers, other homeowners – anyone we thought could help us. Some strategies have worked, some haven't. We have been consistent in our efforts, but ultimately to no avail.

When I read my devotion today, I realized WHAT we, as homeowners, have been missing – is God. That we cannot achieve our goals by our own fleshly efforts no matter WHO we contact; we need God's help to do what needs to be done.

In John 15:5 Jesus says "I am the Vine, you are the branches. When we're joined, the harvest is abundant. Separated, YOU can't produce a thing."

I'm reminded, to seek God in EVERYTHING – even in meetings where you think you have it all together. God Himself IS the success & the victory.

Now, go be Great!

He Didn't Remember His Birthday

I was talking to a friend recently and mentioned I knew his birthday was sometime in December. Well, he told me. It was actually the DAY he and I were on the phone! I was surprised he didn't have anything big planned like he normally does.

He told me he hadn't had time to plan anything special. In fact, he said he almost forgot. Forgot? Kind of like my cousin who I have to remind her of her own birthday! I started thinking – Are we THAT BUSY?? You don't remember your OWN birthday?!

When I read my devotion today it talked about distractions in life – distractions that keep us busy – too busy for God.

Luke 9:62 says "Anyone who lets himself be distracted from the work I plan for him is NOT fit for the Kingdom of God."

I thought do I allow other people, my own hobbies or my past (like guilt, pain) distract me what's important? I'm reminded to let go of distractions, simplify my life & focus on God's mission for me.

Now, go be Great!

I Just Got Approved

I was scrolling through my emails on my phone last night and saw where a store notified me that I was PRE-QUALIFIED to shop with them! That I was APPROVED to spend to a certain amount, of course.

I have to be honest, at first glance I got a little excited seeing the words PREQUALIFIED and APPROVED. And that they'd let me know immediately just how much I'd be approved for. But, I know it's a trap; a trap just to get me into more debt.

During my devotion today, and thought that's the same excitement I should have when I think God has already APPROVED and QUALIFIED me. Like the apostles Peter and John in Acts 4:13 that says they were "ordinary and uneducated", but they were called by God. So I'm reminded, to get excited about being APPROVED by God. Because when He calls me, He qualifies me.

Now, go be Great!

No Way Out, But Through

I was watching a movie last night and a mother was venting to a friend about her daughter's illnesses. The child was wheelchair-bound, couldn't swallow solid food and had to be fed intravenously & among a few things.

The mom's friend asked 'How are you doing with all this?' The mom replied, "Sometimes the only way out is through." I thought about that for a second and realized in my devotion, God never said in life I won't go through. In fact, in

1st Peter 5:10 he says, "After you've suffered a little while, the God of all grace will restore, confirm, strengthen and establish you."

And God says in

Isaiah 43:1- 3 "…when you pass through the waters, I will be with you. And through the rivers, they won't overwhelm you and when you walk thru the fire you won't be burned."

So, I'm reminded in life I WILL face turmoil. I WILL face challenges, but the beauty in that, is knowing it's God who will see me through.

Now, go be Great!

Focusing On The Now

I was busy trying to finalize my Christmas shopping last night and then prepping snacks for our Christmas Eve girlfriend gathering, then organizing gifts to wrap for the next day. Oh, and did I mention finishing up work, stuff too?

By the end of the evening, I was exhausted – not just physically but mentally. It's all the prepping that has me a little anxious now. You know, you want everything to be right.

When I read my devotion today, it brought things into perspective for me.

Matthew 6:34 says "Give your entire attention to what God is doing right NOW and don't get worked up about what may or may not happen tomorrow. God will help you deal with whatever hard things come up when the time comes."

So, I'm reminded stop worrying about all the holiday prep stuff, Janine. Focus on God and focus on NOW.

Now, go be Great!

When You're Caught In The Hustle

I'm happy to say I finished up my Christmas shopping yesterday. Okay. I DECIDED to stop shopping yesterday.

I just stopped and thought – why am I REALLY in the hustle and bustle? I actually CHOSE NOT to let the shopping be important anymore. My devotion yesterday Matthew 6:34 helped, when God says to put all my focus on HIM.

Well, my devotion today further confirmed that. In Luke 10:41-42 when the sisters Mary and Martha invited Jesus for a meal. Mary was chilling with Jesus listening to Him teach. Meanwhile, Martha was running around prepping (like I've been shopping, wrapping, partying), & said to Jesus "Tell her to help me!" Jesus said "You are worried and upset about many things, but few things are needed. Mary has chosen what's better and it won't be taken away from her." That reminded me, I CAN fill my life with GOOD things like at Christmas. But I don't want those THINGS to take away my time with God. I'll focus on what matters most: HIM.

Now, go be Great!

To Plan Or Not To Plan

As I started to prepare for a NEW YEAR – NEW ideas, NEW news for my show. One news story in particular – actress Betty White had died – 2 weeks before her 100th birthday.

I remembered seeing a TV promo of this big birthday party the network was having for her, celebrating her 100th birthday, her 70+ years in the business and still doing it at 99 years old.

But then, she died. I thought, "Wow! All that hoopla and hype and she will NOT be here to see it." A friend said to me, "They (Hollywood) jinxed her with all the planning." I said, "No. It's just a reminder no matter how much planning, prepping, arranging we do, GOD IS IN COMPLETE CONTROL."

Proverbs 19:21 says it. "We humans keep brainstorming options and plans, but God's purpose prevails."

I'm reminded, no one (not even in Hollywood) could stop Betty White from dying." And that as I go into the NEW YEAR, there's nothing NEW about God – He's still in control.

Now, go be Great!

When You Don't Move

Over the holiday, I was driving with my mom. I was at the entrance ramp, about to merge onto the highway. Another car is in front of me. Not moving at all. I'm thinking, can he at least inch up to start merging to get on the highway?

He needed to create momentum. He didn't do that. He literally just sat trying to wait out the traffic. I'm thinking – It's a highway. There's no waiting out traffic to clear. You have to start inching out there to merge with some traffic. He finally did. But, I thought about it later. He got stuck trying to get on the highway.

He didn't move. I thought how many times have I done that in life. I want to get to a destination or achieve a goal, but I'm not moving. I'm not DOING anything. In Hebrews 11:8-10, Abraham said yes to God when he went to an unknown place & had no idea it would become his home. His action was his FAITH. I'm reminded, when I get in stuck in life, start believing in God, ACTIVATE my faith & see what God will do.

Now, go be Great!

Why Am I Running?

The new year has come with excitement for me – new opportunities, both personal and professional (I'll share later). But it's also come with some new challenges – that seem to be growing faster than the opportunities.

Just stuff – from finances, to living space, to family – just stuff. It just makes me say "Okay, God – what's going on?" When I read my devotion today, it was on the prophet Jonah whom God told to go to this big city and preach because the people were really bad off. Jonah went the other direction, totally going away from God. So God sent a huge storm.

Jonah 1:11 says "The storm was getting worse all the time."

It seemed the more Jonah ran, the worse the storm got. I thought is that me? I have these storms brewing, because I'm running from God, like Jonah? I'm reminded, DON'T run from the storms, Janine. Maybe the storms are His way of correcting me and getting me to RUN TOWARDS God instead.

Now, go be Great!

My Bright Lights Are On

I was going to see a friend who leaves basically in the country. By that, I mean NO street lights on the road to her house. I usually have to turn on my bright lights to see, but I turn them off when I see another car so as not to blind them.

Well, as I was driving, another car was approaching me. Of course, we both had on our bright lights. So I dimmed mine so they could see. They never dimmed theirs, so I had to flick mine to cue them and say "Hey, hey - dim your lights so I can see."

During my devotion, I thought about those bright lights. I thought about God. Because HE is the light.

1st John 1:5 says "God is light, pure light. There's not a trace of darkness in him."

I thought, you know I should never have to bring attention to my bright light (like we do with social media sometimes – look at me, see me) & like I did with that other car. I thought If God is light, I walk in Him (being obedient, trusting, have faith), His light shines in me. I'm reminded, if God is in me I won't have to TELL you my brights are on, you'll see it. Just like the bright lights from the other car – I'll shine.

Now, go be Great!

When He's MIA

A girlfriend and I were talking about a new guy she met. They seemed to hit it off really well – until they didn't. He ghosted her. Just went MIA – missing in action. Of course she was disappointed and felt empty.

When I had my devotion today – I had to admit I've had similar feelings – spiritually when it seems God gets missing. Especially in life when things don't go as I planned, or they're disappointments or nothing's happening at all. I feel ghosted by God. My devotion reminded me – not the case. He's there.

In Hebrews 13:5, God says "I will never leave you. I will never abandon you."

Pastor Rick Warren says when it seems God is distant, it's us looking for an experience rather seeking God. And sometimes God removes those FEELINGS so we can't depend on them, but draw closer to Him instead. I'm reminded… God is not MIA or ghosting me. It's my chance to trust & believe & seek Him harder.

Now, go be Great!

Answer Before I Ask

So I had a little cause for concern the other day. I got a call back from radiology saying they noticed something on my mammogram and need a second image.

I did a very small gasp and said "Ok". The clincher is that couldn't get me back in for another two weeks. You know it was on my mind the whole two weeks & I was praying. But deep down, there was also a calmness I had. I believed God had it.

Fast forward, I'm back at radiology; a second image taken & assistant says doctor will join me next to discuss. I'm praying & waiting. Assistant bursts back in and says "No, you're good. Doctor reviewed & says it was just a poor image taken & that I'm clear. She didn't even need to come in to talk to me." I immediately said, 'Thank you, Jesus.' And thought 'that's how you do it? That fast? Like that?' My devotion today answered me.

Isaiah 65:24 says "I will answer them before they even call to Me. While they are still talking about their needs, I will go ahead and answer their prayers."

I'm reminded, keep believing, keep trusting. God's got it.

Now, go be Great!

Strength In The Middle Of Pain

I was waiting on a phone call from my niece who promised to follow up for our weekly talk. She had an assignment due and I wanted to know her progress. Our call was for 7pm. Then 8 came, then 9. Finally, it was the next day. No call from my niece even after she promised.

We've since talked and I shared my disappointment. She apologized and I kept it moving. I thought about my disappointment and her breaking her promise. My devotion today talked about David when he prayed to God because he was afraid for his life.

He complained to God, but he yet he still praised Him, too.

In Psalm 116:10 David wrote, "I believed, so I said I am completely ruined."

It was like a contradiction – I believe in you God, but I CAN'T. Then I thought – David was broken & surrendered, and believed at the same time. An act of deep faith. So, I'm reminded even in the midst of my own turmoil when I complain to God, I will hold on to what I know is true: I can still trust that God is with me. He still loves me and He won't break His promise.

Now, go be Great!

When I Need To Be Quiet

I have been quiet on social media for the past few days. And of course in my business, that's not good. We always have to post something. "Engage your audience" is what the social media experts say. Well, I haven't been.

And to be honest – that 'silence' actually 'revived' me! I realized I was able to use that 'silence' to engage more with God. And it actually strengthened me and I was able to focus more. I enjoyed the silence.

My devotion today – 1st Kings 19:11-12 – when Elijah needed direction from God after his life was threatened. Angels told him to stand on a mountain & wait on God.

Hurricane wind, an earthquake and fire came, but no God. It wasn't until AFTER all the noise passed that Elijah heard God's gentle, quiet whisper. I'm reminded, life is full of noise, like social media, that can keep me from hearing God. But, silence can be louder than noise. Silence is good for my soul and lets me hear the still, small voice of God.

Now, go be Great!

When Your Mind Works Overtime

My cousin and I were talking recently, rather decompressing from planning. More specifically, we'd been planning out my mom's week – from what she'll eat for lunch, dinner, her activities, hair appointments, etc.

Understanding my mom is still extremely independent. She doesn't think she NEEDS ANY help, which makes it more challenging because we have to strategize HOW to help her. Nonetheless, it's exhausting, mentally. Like figuring out when to help, how to help, who's gonna help do what? All while not agitating my mom. Too much!

In my devotion today, though, I realized all that is NOT too much for God.

Proverbs 3:5 says "Lean on, trust in and be confident in the Lord with all your heart and mind. Do NOT rely on your own insight or understanding."

After reading that & letting it soak in – I felt relief. And I was reminded, mental tiredness is a real thing; my mind needs rest, too. And just thank God I DON'T HAVE TO overthink & try to figure it all out. I'll depend on Him instead. God's got it & ready to serve.

Now, go be Great!

When You Have No Control

This winter storm we've had the last few days honestly had me a bit relieved. I knew I'd be home catching up on both rest and work. But, my friend from Chicago didn't think that way. She's in town for business could NOT understand why the city practically shut down for "these few snowflakes" she said.

She was frustrated and told me, "I've got things to do!!" I told her she may as well sit back! Most businesses were closed & there was nothing she could do about it! Relax, I told her.

And when I thought about it…that's something God has told me over and over again when I get anxious. My devotion today emphasized it.

Psalm 46:10 "Let go of your concerns! Then you will know that I AM GOD. I RULE THE NATIONS. I RULE THE EARTH."

I'm reminded I'm NOT in control & to take the same advice I gave my friend 'Sit back, RELAX'. And that there is relief from stress & it starts with letting God be God.

Now, go be Great!

When I Wasn't Feeling It

I told my bestie recently 'I'm not really FEELIN' the love' from you lately. And I said that because where we used to talk more frequently, we weren't talking at all. And I wasn't FEELIN that!

But even though we hadn't connected in a few weeks, when we did it was as if that time passed never happened. We didn't skip a beat. Our conversation & laughter did not change one BIT! Our friendship didn't go away.

And I thought about that later during my devotion. How I got IN MY FEELINGS because my bestie and I hadn't talked. In the book of Job who lost everything in ONE DAY – his family, his business, his health – Job wasn't really FEELIN' GOD and told God he was angry & bitter. But in Job 1:20, 21 ended up praising God even when he thought he was absent & said "The Lord gave and the Lord has taken away. May He be praised."

When it seemed like God was distant, He was there the whole time. (just like my friendship with my bestie) I'm reminded, for God it's NOT about the FEELING, it's about the FAITH in his presence & KNOWING He's there even when I don't FEEL it.

Now, go be Great!

When The Weather Is Whack

When I was watching the weather report for this week, I saw one day it was going to be sunny, in the upper 50's. Didn't I just see ice on my balcony? Then, I saw where in Texas it was expected to be almost 80 degrees & sunny, then an ice storm only 36 hours. I thought about all of that for a minute.

I thought, "Wow! The mighty power of God! How amazing!" Only God could make those kind of dramatic changes. And not just with the weather, but like in my life. Like it can be cloudy, uncertain and scarce in my life one moment, then sun shining, provision & abundance the next. My devotion today

Deuteronomy 28:1 says "If you fully obey the Lord your God and follow all his commands…all these blessings will come on you."

I'm reminded – Janine, just believe in Him, follow Him and know there are NO LIMITS to HIS power. What seems crazy & impossible like the weather changing, is POSSIBLE with God.

Now, go be Great!

When My Battery Is Dead

I grabbed my laptop this morning and turned it on – nothing. The screen was pitch black. Ugh! I was thinking do I REALLY need to go grab the cord and plug it in?? Then I thought "That's the ONLY WAY you're gonna get this computer to work." The battery is dead & it needs power.

Of course I plugged it in and voila – my laptop lit up & was working again. I started thinking again. Such a simple concept. Laptop battery dead, plug it in to recharge.

I thought that's how my relationship with God works – sort of. When I find myself worried, anxious or even fearful…I'm not really working well like my laptop – that's because I've NOT been plugged into my source – God. My laptop wasn't working because I forgot to charge the battery. But, I'm reminded if I stay plugged into God AT ALL TIMES, I'll stay charged & have ALL the POWER I need.

Now, go be Great!

I Got Distracted

I have a confession. I made a mistake during one of my inspirational moments last week. I accidentally re-read an inspiration I had done the day before. Not a terribly bad thing, but I was so mad at myself. How could I do that? What happened??

And I know what happened. Normally, I have to have my "quiet time" right before my moment. But I was preoccupied. I was not focused on God. I was focused on interruptions in the room, people talking, I was talking, phone buzzing, music loud etc. Everything was pulling my attention away from my "moment" with God. So I made that mistake.

I thought about that moment later and realized that's so much like in life, Janine.

Sometimes, I allow things, people, thoughts, behaviors to interfere with my moment with God. I know there will be interruptions that pull me away from Him. And when I take my eyes off of God, things will fall apart like Peter sinking in Matthew 14. So I'm reminded of Hebrews 12:2 to keep my eyes fixed on Jesus. My faith comes from Him and He's the One who makes it perfect.

Now, go be Great!

What's My Money Plan?

I am proud of myself lately because I've really started to be more conscious about my finances. Don't get me wrong, I've always thought about how and where I spend my money, but not really putting it into practice. I've had a budget, but never really followed it – until now.

I don't know why now – maybe it's being 50 something. Or maybe I'm not too far off from retirement. But either way, I think God is nudging me to be prepared. With the whole squirrel fiasco – squirrels prepare for winter – and my devotions lately have focused on money. Like today –

Proverbs 14:8 says "The wise man looks ahead. The FOOL attempts to fool himself and won't face facts."

And in Luke 16… the businessman who was dishonest, but God commended him because he had a plan & planned ahead. Here I've been thinking God doesn't care about my money. Not true. I'm reminded he doesn't want me to hoard it, or worship my money, but rather as it says in

Proverbs 16:9 – "I should make plans and count on God to direct me".

Now, go be Great!

To Post Or Pray

I was listening recently to a social media strategist and how social media has changed the landscape in our society. For example, for broadcasters like me, we HAVE to engage listeners OFF the air as much as we do ON the air.

The strategist said name of the game is social media. And in almost any profession or business, it's part of the job. If you want to be seen – you GOTTA do social media & consistently. But this morning, I didn't want my 'posting or blogging' to get in the way of my God time.

1st John 2: 15-17 confirmed it shouldn't. It says "Don't love the world's ways. Don't love the world's goods. Love of the world squeezes out love for the Father. Everything that goes on in the world – WANTING your own way, WANTING everything for yourself, WANTING to appear important, has NOTHING to do with the Father. It just isolates you from HIM."

I want to do my job & post on social media, but I'm reminded not let my posting get in the way of my praying. What God wants comes first.

Now, go be Great!

When I'm Not Active

I had the TV on the other day, but not watching it. After a while, a message popped up on the TV that said something like – Please click any button on remote to keep TV active then it started a countdown when it would turn off the TV.

I'd seen that message before. Anyway, I clicked a button and it continued to show the program that was on. I thought these smart TVs. Then I thought – they are really smart. It's wired to realize the TV has been inactive and checking to see if I'm still there, so it prompts me with a message.

Sounds familiar. I believe God does that with me sometimes when I'm INACTIVE with Him. He nudges me, gives me a message. In my devotion today,

Psalm 27: 13, 14 says "I'll see God's goodness in the earth. Stay with God! Don't quit. Stay with God."

I realize when my TV is on and I'm away, it can send me a message, prompting me to be active, but so does God. Except God wants my faith active, wants my trust in Him active. And when I stray, I'm reminded to GET BACK TO GOD. GET BACK TO GOD.

Now, go be Great!

Understanding The Assignment

Every now and then I'll listen to some hip-hop on the radio. Like young folk hip-hop. Anyway, I heard this song and the hook was "I understood the assignment." I'd heard it before…kind of catchy. And that's the name of the song "The Assignment."

I found myself singing the hook throughout the day. And strangely enough, I thought about that hook during my devotion today. 2nd Corinthians: 7-10 when Paul talks about the man with a handicap he thought he had to help him stay grounded. And how he asked God to remove it, but realized the handicap was really a gift. He started to understand his assignment.

Because God then said 'My grace is enough. It's all you need. My strength comes into its own in your weakness.' So I'm reminded in that verse no matter my limitations – accidents, opposition, bad breaks – I need to just let God take over! So, the weaker I get, the stronger I become. And that's when I can REALLY say "I understand the assignment."

Now, go be Great!

What Am I Investing In?

My cousin and I have been talking investments lately. We are determined to actively pursue interests that can contribute to a solid financial future. In other words, we want to make sure our money is right down the road.

In doing that, we are now investing in stocks. Of course, we had to get educated first. What to invest in, how much, how it works, etc. My financial advisor says the money won't necessarily roll in overnight, but that it's an investment that takes time.

I thought about the time I've been taking to look into stocks & planning my financial future…but after my devotion today, I thought Janine are you taking the same amount of care & diligence investing in God? How much time have I taken to seek Him? I'm reminded investing in my finances for my future is SMART, but investing in my spiritual life, seeking God above all is NECESSARY. Seek God first, Janine, the rest will follow.

Now, go be Great!

When Your Vision Gets Blurry

So, I'm cooking a new recipe last night. Of course, I grab my readers because the print is blurry. As I start to review the recipe with my readers, it's still blurry. I'm rubbing my eyes, trying to refocus and I STILL can't see clearly. I do a semi panic and think "Wait a minute, am I losing my sight?"

As it turns out, the lens of my readers are greasy and dirty – THAT'S why my vision was blurred. Later, I thought about my mini-moment of panic and how my vision was a little blurry, I automatically went to thinking the worse.

During my devotion today, I thought that's how do in life sometimes – think the worst like in Numbers 14:1-2 when the Israelites responded to negative reports of the Promised Land, "Then the whole community began weeping, they cried all night" and even said 'If only we had died in Egypt.' I thought – Boy was THEIR vision blurred too. They wanted death instead of looking ahead? I'm reminded of

Philippians 4:19 "And my God will meet all your needs according to the riches of his glory".

I don't want my vision of the future blurred by fear, instead I want it to be lead by faith.

Now, go be Great!

My Delivery Is Delayed

I got a notice via text and my email that always makes me happy! It was an update from Amazon letting me know the package I ordered is on its way! I ordered it several weeks ago and because of all the supply chain issues, there were several delays, but it's finally almost here!

In fact, my package is scheduled to arrive! YAY! During my devotion today, I thought about my excitement over getting my package – that's the same excitement and expectancy I should have with God.

Zechariah 4:6 says "Not by might nor by power, but by Your Spirit, oh God."

Which says to me only God has the POWER to turn things around in my life – a shift that man CANNOT create. So, I'm reminded even when there are delays, Janine, like your Amazon package, I should still remain excited, believe, expect and have FAITH that God still has blessings for me that are on the way.

Now, go be Great!

When Is It Going To Happen?

My cousin and I have been putting off having a conversation with my brother about a family matter. We both know he can be a bit intense, so we knew it mattered when and how we discussed it. AND we wanted his wife present, too.

Anyway, we've put it off now for a couple of weeks struggling to figure out when we were all gonna be free at the same time. Our schedules didn't line up. But, we both prayed about it. How about the conversation happened and without our coordination.

My cousin & I were on the phone, my brother beeped in. He was with his wife. I connected all of us. We talked. And just like that – it was done. And I shouldn't be surprised. Because when I read my devotion today that's what God does.

Isaiah 60:22 says "I am God. At the right time, I will make it happen."

So, I'm reminded, Janine no matter what IT is – relationship, promotion, health report – in due season God WILL make it happen. I'll just have FAITH and THANK HIM for the blessing.

Now, go be Great!

I Love You, But...

I don't know if you've ever had to care for a parent, but if you have you know it's a FULL TIME job! And it zaps you of most of your energy, not just physically but mentally and emotionally.

Of course, I absolutely LOVE my mom and there's not anything I wouldn't do for her. But, if I'm being honest it was hard making it back home this past weekend. I was exhausted, had my own work to do & wasn't in the mental headspace. But of course I went and DID NOT regret it.

When I read my devotion today, I realize I'm a reluctant servant & I can be selfish. I had to admit I sometimes say – I love you, Lord, BUT. But there is no but. God wants me to serve Him with all my heart & joyfully by ministering to others like my mom. I realize service is never convenient and may mean giving up my comfort. But, Hebrews 13:21 reminded me, God promises to equip me with everything good for doing His will. I'm also reminded my serving God is not in vain.

Now, go be Great!

To Do Or Not To Do

Yesterday evening I did not feel like doing my daily walk – at all. I really wanted to take a nap, but something kept nagging me 'Janine, just get it in.' So I did. Then a cousin whom I hardly ever talk to – maybe twice a year – called me out of the blue. She needed to borrow money. At first I hesitated, but then something in me said "Do it!" So I did.

When I had my devotion today, it confirmed what I already know. When my head is telling me one thing, but my heart is saying something else? It's something deep inside me urging me to do it another way – that it's God trying to guide me.

Proverbs 4: 6-7 says 'Never walk away from wisdom. She guards your life. Love her. She keeps her eye on you.'

So, I'm reminded when I'm making a decision with my head, but get that tugging in my heart, know that's the Holy Spirit urging me to walk in wisdom and I'll trust Him.

Now, go be Great!

Learning To Swim

I was watching a TV show last night in which a husband and wife were in a lake and he was teaching her how to float. She didn't know how to swim. His instructions were simple. Just lay back until the water touches your ears, lift your legs, and trust me – I got you.

She was as stiff as a board. And seeing that wife struggle to float reminded me of MY experience in swimming. Trying to float when you can't swim -- you can't relax, you think you're gonna go under, you think you're gonna drown. Which really says you DON'T TRUST the person to 'have you.'

I had all the negative thoughts. In my mind all the conditions were there for me to drown. Like in life when things aren't right (bills, health, family, job). But my devotion today says God doesn't want us to ignore our circumstances; He wants us to control our negative thinking and say "I may have problems, but God is with me." So I'm reminded – like learning to swim, I gotta learn to lean back, let go and TRUST GOD's got me.

Now, go be Great!

Let Me Do This First

When I got up this morning, as usual I start to pray and do my devotion. But, I had so many distractions. My phone was pinging, one after another. But, not a big deal because I've learned to silence it and stick to my plan – DO MY DEVOTION FIRST.

Because I had a laundry list of things to GET DONE, in my head…I kept thinking BEFORE my devotion, let me just do this one thing. (let me make this one quick call, return this one quick email, respond to this one text). Until I literally had to say out loud to myself, "No maam…DO YOUR DEVOTION!"

So I did. And THAT was my devotion.

Matthew 6:33 "Seek ye FIRST the kingdom of God and His righteousness & all these things shall be added to you."

My inspiration – Don't allow outside energies &, distractions to interfere with my time with God. I was reminded, very clearly, DO GOD FIRST – period.

Now, go be Great!

I'm Still Here

Today marks my work anniversary. It was 28 years ago that I arrived in Charlotte not knowing I'd still be working here. In fact, it was my plan to stay here no more than five years…but God.

MY plan was to get as much radio experience as possible and then BOUNCE. But, a lot of what I've done was NOT MY PLAN. Like starting a nonprofit, leading a board, becoming a fundraiser, work mornings at a hip-hop station, leave the station then come back as a full-time personality with my OWN show.

So, when I read my devotion today – it all made sense.

Proverbs 16:9 says "We Plan the way we want to live, but only God makes us able to live it."

I realize none of what I PLANNED was MY doing – including my staying in Charlotte 23 years more than I planned. I'm reminded while I wanted to be here, ultimately it was God's doing – giving me the ability & making it possible for me to stay.

Now, go be Great!

But That's Not Me

I was reviewing my show prep. You know, things I planned to talk about on air. One of those things was the racial discrimination lawsuit a black head coach was pursuing against the NFL. I took a few notes on it, but I didn't plan to go deep because I knew my partner, QCB the sports guy would cover it.

So we talked about it on air and it was fine. But, later I thought about my not wanting to go too deep into sports. It's just NOT my wheelhouse. That's NOT what I do. But, should I?

During my devotion today, I read a note I had written from TD Jakes who said 'stay focused on the assignment. Stop trying to operate in a place where God didn't put you. ' And I thought, Janine – God DID NOT make you a sports enthusiast, so don't pretend to be. And that applies not just in sports, but in life. Hebrews 13:21 says God equips me with everything good for doing His will. So, I'm reminded God wants me to be who he's deemed me to be to fulfill the work He's called me to do & it doesn't require faking it. Because what His gift is already in me.

Now, go be Great!

What Do I Get?

Now that Valentine's Day is over, I started thinking about how much people spend on that one day to celebrate love. I read that in the U.S., people spent 24 BILLION dollars for Valentine's Day.

And the average person would spend about $200 on their significant other. Either way, that's a lot of love for ONE day in February! I thought 'What about the other days?'

Then I read my devotion – 1st Corinthians 13:4 talks all about love and what it's NOT. Love never gives up. It doesn't strut or have a swelled head or force itself on others. It isn't always me first. Love DOES always look for the best and keeps going to the end.

And Love trusts God. So, I'm reminded I can spend tons of money on a significant other on Valentine's Day or even send gifts to my closest friends, but none of that matters if I don't have love in it. God is reminding me that's the BEST gift of them all — LOVE.

Now, go be Great!

When The Hardest Thing To Do Is The Right Thing

I was on the phone recently with a girlfriend who's been sick & now has an infection that's affecting her breathing. Her doctor recommended she stay home and in bed until her oxygen levels normalize.

But, of course since she's so used to moving around and making things pop, staying still is a real challenge for her. So, I asked her do you think God is creating this opportunity for you to sit still on purpose? She thought, then admitted she had been putting off working on her book.

I probed more. Then she said her real reason for procrastinating was fear of what emotions writing the book would drum up in her. Then I told her what someone told me recently – the very thing you're challenged in doing, that nagging thing you keep putting off, is likely the Holy Spirit wanting to use you (your story, your pain) to help someone else & by NOT doing it, you're being selfish. I realized I was preaching to myself and was reminded – Janine, God wants to USE me, too to be a blessing to others & ultimately for His glory.

Now, go be Great!

Who Do I Run To?

I was walking along the greenway yesterday with a friend when apparently I walked right through a bunch of gnats. I didn't notice them at first, but as I continued to walk I could see them hovering around my head. I thought if I walked faster, they'd move & I could get away from them. It didn't work.

They continued to hover around my face and head. Then I started to run, thinking I could out pace them. It seemed the more I tried to dodge those gnats, the more they hovered.

It reminded me of times I've been that way with God – trying to dodge His will or run away from what He's has for me. Starting the nonprofit Girl Talk or delivering these inspirational moments even. Neither one I really wanted to do, so I'd run from them. My devotion today

Matthew 6:32 & 33 says "…God knows your needs. RUN for his kingdom & everything that you need will be taken care of."

I'm reminded, Janine don't try to out-run God, instead RUN to HIM to fulfill His purpose for your life.

Now, go be Great!

When Someone Needs You

I got a phone call the other day from a relative – a young cousin who needed to borrow some money. She explained she came up short this month and needed to pay a bill and get some groceries.

I can honestly say I didn't hesitate to help her. Now, I did double-check my account, but once I saw I was good, I sent her a decent amount. And I actually felt good about myself. She said she'd pay me back, but in my head – I wasn't expecting it. It was okay.

When I had my devotion today, I realized my giving so freely with no regret is how I'm supposed to be to my neighbor when they are dealing with adversity. Jesus set the example in

Matthew 11:28 & 29 when He said… "Come to Him, if you're weary and burdened, He'll give you rest."

I'm reminded I can't wait for MY life to be good before I can help others. God wants me to help hold somebody else up & when I do I'm fulfilling God's command to love my neighbor as I love myself.

Now, go be Great!

From Messy To Masterpiece

I know a lot of people are upset that my radio brother Tone X no longer works here at the station. I am, too! It hurts. It's confusing. It's shocking, even, asking 'where did this come from?' My head says 'It's, business, JD'…while my heart says 'It's not fair, it's messy & it sucks.'

But, when I read my devotion today – the answer to my question 'where did Tone being released come from?' – was there… in Romans 8:28 that says 'And we know that in ALL things God works for the good of those who love Him, who have been called according to HIS purpose." So Tone getting released didn't 'just happen'; God orchestrated it. My question was also answered in

Psalm 37: 23 & 24, that says "The Lord directs the steps of the godly. He delights in EVERY detail of their lives. Though they stumble, they will never fall, the Lord holds them by hand."

So, I'm reminded when things in life happen that catch me off guard, like Tone getting released from his radio job, that God is the ultimate programmer who I WILL TRUST and who can turn a messy situation into a masterpiece.

Now, go be Great!

When I Feel Trapped

I've been talking with a girlfriend recently who has been in pursuit of a new home to get out of her apartment, but has had no luck. Then FINALLY she calls to tell me she found "the one".

It had everything she wanted. A bit pricey, but she could make it work. She signed the necessary paperwork. I was thrilled for her.

A few days later we talked, I asked what's up with the house. She said the deal fell through. It's NOT going to happen. She was devastated. I said, 'That just wasn't "the one." Then I said, just like God got you a new job, a big promotion – just let Him do this, too.

When I read my devotion today – Exodus 14 when God saved the Israelites from the Egyptians by holding back the sea…so the Israelites were able to travel on dry ground. Then God caused the sea to go back in place & drowned the Egyptians. I imagine the Israelites thought they had no way out, were trapped & doomed, like my friend looking for her house. But verse 14 says

"The Lord will fight for you, you only need to be still."

So I'm reminded, God is capable & creative. He CAN make a way out of no way like He always does.

Now, go be Great!

I'm Worthy

My girlfriend is being courted by a company. One that she's ignored for a couple of years because she likes her job, she's doing well FINANCIALLY, so she's good. Or so she thought. She finally talked to the other company – THEY are offering to pay her at least DOUBLE of what she's currently making.

She had no clue. Another friend just got a new gig. She told me the benefits are unbelievable. There's a full-scale gym and a cafeteria with healthy food that you can also order to take home for you AND your family. I was like 'WOW'! Then I thought WE DESERVE THIS!!

So why do I sometimes settle & think 'I'm good right here.' Not, when there's a God, Janine. My devotion

Isaiah 55:1, 2 backs that up "…All who are thirsty, come to the water! Eat only the best, fill yourself with only the finest."

God did that for David – made him a prince & a leader of nations that never even heard of him, but they came running because of God. So I'm reminded, I don't have to settle. The gifts of God are abundant, they're the best and available to me. I just need to know to, SEEK GOD and BELIEVE I'm worth it!

Now, go be Great!

Stop Fighting

A good girlfriend's mom just died recently. But, before she passed, my friend's mom had an 'episode' and my friend had to revive her. She never fully regained consciousness, but yet all her vitals were normal.

My friend would later explain her mom wouldn't let go. She continued to fight to breathe. Once all her kids surrounded her, she passed – peacefully.

At the wake, I saw her face. The ultimate look of peace – even a slight smile. I thought about her mom's fighting spirit & thought Janine, this is the look, the spirit you can have when you stop fighting God in life here on earth, and just surrender. Like when He asks me to do something I don't want to do or something happens I don't like, stop fighting, Janine – with fighting there's pain, discomfort, confusion. So, I'm reminded when I let go of that fear, the pride & just surrender…Let God lead I'll get the peace He has waiting for me.

Now, go be Great!

I Choose

I was reviewing a book I bought a few years ago. It's Don Miguel Ruiz's book 'The Four Agreements'. It's four simple 'beliefs' to live by to simplify your life. I was focused on the second agreement that says " Don't Take Anything Personally".

Ruiz essentially says when you take things personally, you're CHOOSING to believe something about yourself that is likely NOT true. He says when you take something personally, YOU choose to take on that's person's belief, that person's poison. It's a CHOICE you're making.

My devotion today talked about choices. That everyday when we wake up, we can CHOOSE to trust God. In fact, it says that's how I eliminate stress in my life because with DAILY FAITH, there's no room for worry or stress. Choosing FAITH EVERYDAY drives away fear. So I'm reminded just like I can CHOOSE or not CHOOSE to take things personally, I can and will CHOOSE FAITH in God EVERY DAY to meet ALL my needs.

Now, go be Great!

Never Left

I was up late –just scrolling through social media. I had just been sitting in the quiet, meditating and thinking about God and how He plans to use me. And wondering, quite honestly, had I been praying the right prayer or praying enough and DOING enough to hear from Him.

I'm thinking all this as I scroll through social media and ran across a conversation from a local minister – shout out to Pastor Nicole Martin. She was talking about how we try to get BACK in God's good graces when we think we haven't been. We beg, we plead, and sometimes bargain.

But, she says that's not how God works. I sometimes think God's missing or I need to DO something to get God back like when I was questioning God earlier. But the fact is God never leaves. He's always there and I need to remember that. So, I'm reminded instead of asking or pleading with God, I should be thanking and praising Him for the ALL the goodness He's already sent my way and will send my way. So, I just say – thank you GOD!

Now, go be Great!

Hands Off The Wheel

Have you ever just been stressed and it's not just ONE thing. It's a multitude – work, home, family, more work. And yes, I pray and yes, I have my devotion but sometimes it just gets overwhelming.

That was me yesterday. But then it changed after ONE simple task I did afterwork. I got my car washed. In my car, I put it in neutral as instructed by the attendee, took my foot off the accelerator, hands off the steering wheel, leaned back & just sat there.

And I forgot just how calming it was – and how necessary. I reflected back on another time at the car wash when I was in that same mode of relief, no control, no decision- making, hands-free…and I was reminded that's just how God wants me to be when I RELAX in in Him, when I TRUST Him. Thank you, God for reminding me to take my hands off the wheel.

Now, go be Great!

An Unexpected Blessing

Normally, I go LIVE on my Facebook page three days a week dancing during the mix show. The other two days, I recuperate. Nonetheless, I went LIVE on a day I don't normally go LIVE.

I did not plan on it, but there I was live and dancing. Members of my tribe or the Hunni Hive is what I call it, started to join. One of the Hunni Hive members who's recovering from surgery, made a comment. She said "This made my day. This is an unexpected blessing."

I later thought about her comment and thought isn't that how God works? He can drop a blessing when you least expect it. God is in the blessing business.

Philippians 4:19 & 20 says it. "And God will supply every need of yours according to His riches in glory of Christ."

So I'm reminded, no matter what stress I experience – like my friend who's uncomfortable from surgery – God can flip it and create an unexpected blessing.

Now, go be Great!

I Can't Stop It

Had dinner with my cousin and her significant other over the weekend and he asked me 'what was my financial strategy for the next 5 years' which also included some of my career goals.

I shared what I thought was a pretty definitive and well thought out plan. Anyway, we moved on. But, during my devotion I thought about a word yesterday I got listening to Pastor Joel Osteen – who said something I knew, but whatever reason it really hit different yesterday.

Osteen said you cannot change God's sovereign will. He said God will allow me to make my plans, set goals (like my financial and career strategy), but once He decides what is supposed to be, it will be. No matter if I want it (aka start a nonprofit), if I plan it (host a midday radio show) or even set a goal (offer inspirational moments) – and no , I didn't plan any of that. But God did. So, I'm reminded God is way ahead of me & my planning, so no need to stress over what will be. If it's God's will – IT WILL BE & I cannot change it or stop it.

Now, go be Great!

I Can And I Will

I have an upcoming trip out of the country. It IS work-related, but it'll be fun too. In preparation for the trip, a co-worker who is also going discussed my interviews.

I'm thinking – oh boy, that means potential stress from the board operator back here in the states. I was thinking, 'please don't let it be like one other time, when the board op had no idea what she was doing. And I was fed up, and remembered saying I CAN'T and I WON'T!!

I mean I had three more hours of show to do. Anyway, I remember my co worker there with me very calmly said to me – You CAN and You WILL. I took a beat and calmed down. That simple affirmation made the difference. It calmed me. Just like God does when I'm out of sorts & take a beat…He comforts me. Gets me through. Because HE CAN and HE WILL. So I'm reminded in

Matthew 19:26 "Humanly speaking, it's impossible. But with God everything is possible."

Now, go be Great!

He Never Takes A Break

I've been working diligently to better manage my finances. And of course, I've prayed asking God to help me make wise financial decisions.

But, as soon as I try to do right, emergencies pop up. I need to replace my kitchen faucet or time for my car to get serviced. Then I start to think, 'Okay, God. I thought you were helping me.'

And then as I talked about last week – an unexpected blessing. Opening my mail & almost a $1k check in escrow surplus. So I paused when I read my devotion today --

Isaiah 64:4 says "The Lord is a God of action…."

Even when he rested on the seventh day it wasn't because he was tired. He never ceased working. He's always controlling the universe. And at the same time, intimately involved in my life. So, I'm reminded even when you don't see it, Janine -- God is always working on my behalf. Trust Him.

Now, go be Great!

My Story Started Different

I was speaking to an interviewer recently giving her some of my backstory. She was a bit surprised when I shared I was shy as a kid. In fact, I dropped out of kindergarten. I was afraid to be around people.

Fast forward today – a radio personality, in front of people all the time. The interviewer asked me how did that happen? How was that possible? I told her, "God."

I thought about that question during my devotion - How was that possible to be a shy kid afraid of people, then become a brass & sassy radio personality?

Luke 1:37 answered it "For there is nothing that God cannot do."

It doesn't matter how impossible a situation may seem.

Philippians 1:6 confirmed "he who began a good work in you will carry it on to completion."

So, I'm reminded NOTHING is impossible with God.

Now, go be Great!

Did She Get The Job?

A friend shared some good news with me yesterday. She finally got this state job she's been wanting for a while. She actually interviewed for it last December. And all this time – we were both praying, waiting and then more praying.

We were both on an emotional rollercoaster. One minute hopeful (we heard she was in the top 2), then not (heard somebody else got the job) Until finally, we both agreed 'let's practice what WE preach and NOT WORRY.' And claim 'this job is yours.'

And now three months later – it is. The exact job she'd been praying for, the benefits, the salary. EVERYTHING. My devotion today

Jeremiah 33:9 says when God rebuilt Judah & Jerusalem and said "… they'll get reports on all the good I'm doing for her. They'll be in aw of the blessings I am pouring on her."

So, I'm reminded God has great things on the way for me & my friend. He will restore what was lost and command increase. I will RECEIVE IT, EXPECT IT and THANK YOU for my blessings.

Now, go be Great!

When My Hands Are Full

I was juggling a lot in my hands the other day. I had just gotten back from the grocery store – so I had groceries. I had luggage from an overnight trip, my purse, etcetera. AND I was only trying to make that one trip to the car.

I was thinking 'how am I going do this?' BUT, I had it all in my arms, on my shoulder, hands. I'd gotten to the door of my building & thought 'how am I going to open the door?'

And just as I thought that, someone was coming OUT and held the door for me. And I thanked them profusely and thought 'they were right on time'.

I thought about that exchange during my devotion today and how it was so much like life sometimes. Me – trying to juggle everything on my own. And God – coming to my rescue. In fact it's when I'm at my wits end, my weakest is when He does His best work. And God says in

1st Peter 5:7 "to cast on my burdens on Him because He cares."

So, I'm reminded every time I try to 'juggle it all', take a step back, invite God in. And let HIM carry my burdens for me.

Now, go be Great!

When Fear Drives You

I was talking to a friend about doing something she is utterly afraid to do – getting therapy. I heard myself tell her, the best way to get over fear is to do the thing that scares you anyway.

And went on to ask her – 'What's the worst thing that could happen?' And that thing YOU believe can happen is in YOUR head and it's a lie. As I was talking to her, I was preaching to myself about my own hang-ups.

Then during my devotion, I read John 16:33. When Jesus said, "even though the world has trials and tribulations, stress and frustration, we can have perfect peace in Him. For He has overcome the world." He's done it – taken the power away that will harm me like fear & has given me courage. So, I'm reminded it's NOT the problems that bother me, it's how I respond to them. NO need to worry or fear…I choose to have the PEACE and CONFIDENCE He's given me to make it through, no matter what comes against me.

Now, go be Great!

Believe Anyway

On the phone with a friend trying to convince her to keep moving forward on her new venture of jewelry making. She says it's been a passion for her & a God-given talent. So, she's finally doing it.

The thing is—she doesn't really promote it. And I encouraged her and reminded her of her goal – make extra money doing something she loves. But my friend was so doubtful that it won't work?' I thought about my friend's doubt during my devotion today. And honestly, I was a little disappointed.

Then I thought – God probably feels the same way…when I don't believe in Him. When I have doubt. John 20: 24-29 talks about the Apostle Thomas who didn't believe Jesus resurrected until he SAW Him.

In Verse 29 Jesus told Thomas, "… so you believe because you've SEEN with your own eyes. Even better blessings are in store for those who believe WITHOUT seeing."

So I'm reminded, I don't have to SEE to believe. God wants my faith, to remove the doubt and BELIEVE anyway.

Now, go be Great!

I'm Reminded To Do My Job

A local business has been in the news over a dispute regarding a parking lot. Essentially, this business owner doesn't want to share the parking lot with another business – that's African American owned. Even went so far to put up signs that say the parking is for HIS patrons only.

I said the other day – no good can come from this man or his business treating people this way. I thought later about my comment during my devotion. I thought what I said goes for me, too.

In fact 1st Peter 3:12 says I'm to be "agreeable, sympathetic, loving, compassionate and humble. No exceptions. No retaliation."

It says, I am to bless. That blessing is my job. And when I do, I'll be a blessing and also get a blessing." And lastly, the verse says God likes when we do good, but "turns his back on those who do evil things." So, I'm reminded -- Janine , do your job everyday – and everyday find a way to be blessing.

Now, go be Great!

Don't Jump Off

I had the oddest dream last night. I was riding a skateboard. Not so odd because I DO KNOW HOW to ride a skateboard. I used to do it in high school. Anyway, I'm on this skateboard on the sidewalk and it's all these peaks and valleys, curves and swerves.

And I had picked up speed. And I recall when I used to skateboard, when you're in the groove, you don't stop; you go with it. And even though in my dream, I kept picking up speed – it was kind of scary - I never stopped. Then suddenly I did. I was at my destination unharmed.

I thought about my riding the skateboard during my devotion – and the message I got from God was clear. Don't stop Janine. 1st Thessalonians 5:24 says God is faithful, trustworthy and he will do just what He said. Life can be bumpy, and uncertain & scary at times – just like my riding that skateboard. But God reminded me don't jump off. Keep going. He will make sure I make it through.

Now, go be Great!

When The Waves Are Good

I follow this professional surfer by the name of Dominique Miller – this sassy AfroLatina who is a beast on a surf board. She posted a video the other day of her actually trying to surf when there were no big waves. The ocean water was just kind of still.

In her post, she asked a question – Do you surf only when the waves are good? Or do you surf when waves are bad? Dominique says she likes to surf in all conditions – it makes her a more well-rounded surfer.

I thought about that during my devotion – my faith. Do I only have faith when things are good and do I still have faith when things get a bit rocky.

James 1:16 says "But let him ask in faith, nothing wavering. For he that wavereth is like a wave of the sea driven with the wind and tossed.

So, I'm reminded be like the surfer Dominique with my faith – whether the waves in life are good or bad, I won't let my faith waver. I'll stick with God and believe in Him & his word.

Now, go be Great!

When Am I Gonna Let Go

I texted a girlfriend who's been in charge of my Yasssss Hunni merchandise. I wanted to get an update on a recent order and see if she'd reached out to a few clients who were waiting on their orders.

To be honest, her response stung a bit: 'Of course, I will. Don't I always? This time will be no different, but if you want you can do it.' And THIS is the part that really STUNG. She said, 'You MUST TRUST ME. It's been a year.'

So what I needed to hear. I've been down this road before – with God. I explained to my friend that I've always managed my affairs so it was difficult to let go & that I'm working on it. God was saying to me in her response, 'How many more times do I have to PROVE to you, you can TRUST me?' So, my friend helped remind me 'stop trying to MANAGE IT ALL, LET GO, Janine. TRUST GOD with EVERYTHING – period.

Now, go be Great!

I'm Gonna Need A Team

I was talking to a friend about starting her new business. She's not a fan of social media so I told her she'd have to add that to her list of things to do. SHE seemed stressed and said, I'll just have to have someone do that for me.

We both chuckled and agreed that having a great 'team' does help. When I had my devotion today I thought about the conversation I had with my girlfriend. And her saying she'd have someone do social media for her. My devotion reminded me – that's God job.

Proverbs 16:3 says simply, "Put God in charge of your work, then what you've planned will take place."

I thought I'm just like my girlfriend starting her business, putting too much pressure on myself to make sure all things are aligned, build a team, find the right people. And I remember building Girl Talk, when I trusted God, the right person ALWAYS came, like my new Exec Dir. God is reminding me – yes, DO the work Janine. But, let HIM manage it. Then, WATCH THE MAGIC happen.

Now, go be Great!

When Are You Leaving That Parking Space?

So I'm outside a store the other day waiting for this driver to move out of this good parking space that was near the front of the store. Anyway, I put on my signal to let them know I'm waiting for them to move out of the space.

They DON'T move! They are just sitting there. So I'm thinking – don't you see me waiting? Then after about 2 minutes (which seemed like forever), I just moved on. When I did – I was able to grab another 'good parking space' that was even closer.

That simple event popped in my head during my devotion today that talked about NOT moving beyond past pain -- staying parked in pain. I've done that like with my dad. Not letting go and staying in the hurt that he caused us years ago. But staying parked (like that driver in the good space) isn't healing me, God can.

Isaiah 53:4 & 5 says "God took the punishment and that made us whole. Through His bruises we get healed. God has piled all our sins, everything we've done wrong on Him."

So I'm reminded I don't have to stay parked in pain. God can move me forward, heal and restore me.

Now, go be Great!

Surrender To The Struggle

A good friend is in mourning right now. She lost her mom unexpectedly. I don't even know what to begin to say to her and I cannot imagine her grief.

A mutual friend of ours has been with her for the past few days – helping her manage day to day – literally. For example the mutual friend told the grieving friend ' this hour we eat and nap. That's the plan.' My grieving friend repeated it and said 'I have to have a NEW plan, don't I?'

Of course I've been praying for my grieving friend and me, too -- I'm grieving for her. And my devotion today was right on time.

Matthew 5:4 says "Blessed are those who mourn, for they will be comforted."

I thought there's NOTHING comforting about mourning, but I realize it's in that grief God wants me to surrender to Him. So I think I'll tell my friend go ahead and cry – even wallow in the grief. I'll remind her when you surrender, relax in, rest and settle into the way of God, then you begin to experience HIS awesome & deep comfort. Surrender to the struggle.

Now, go be Great!

Made in the USA

Charlotte, NC

May 2023

ABOUT THE AUTHOR

JANINE DAVIS or "JD, the Diva" as most of her listeners know her as has been called 'radio royalty' in the Carolinas. This Greensboro native has built her brand around enriching, empowering and evoking change in community. She's spent much of her radio career in the Queen City of Charlotte. To know "JD" is also to know "The Diva" – spicy, bold and highly energetic radio and TV personality. She holds down the highly rated midday shift (10am – 3pm) heard by thousands each weekday at V 101.9. She is an award-winning 30+ year radio news and entertainment journalist.

As a social impact entrepreneur, JD is highly regarded in the community after creating a nonprofit organization, Girl Talk Foundation, Inc. (Girl Talk), that hosts structured programs to develop girls' (ages 11-16) self-awareness, self-management and social competence. Janine started Girl Talk in 2003 after having candid conversations with young girls. That led to a series of 'real girl talk' (no parent) sessions. Since it's inception, the Foundation has served more than 30,000 girls and their families. Girl Talk Foundation, Inc. continues to thrive under new leadership. A former Girl Talk participant now leads (Alyssa Shepard) the charge.

Janine is a proud member of Delta Sigma Theta Sorority, Inc. and unapologetically shouts "AGGIE PRIDE" in support of her alma mater N.C. A&T State University.

Janine lives by the motto: "Once you discover your greatness, you can be greater than great."

JanineDavis.com

Follow Janine - Facebook, Instagram and Twitter @jddiva
And on TikTok @jddiva_official